Making Flower Children

Sybille Adolphi

Making Flower Children

Floris Books

Translated by Anna Cardwell
Photographs by Wolpert & Strehle, Stuttgart
Illustrations by Böttcher & Bayer, Stuttgart

First published in German as *Blumenkinder für den Jahreszeitentisch*
by Verlag Freies Geistesleben in 1999
First published in English in 2005 by Floris Books, Edinburgh
Second edition 2008

British Library CIP data available

ISBN 978-086315-650-2

Printed in Poland

Contents

For Has, Benjamin and Nelia

Introduction

The seasonal tableau, or season table, has a firm place in our home and family.

It is made of natural materials like moss, branches, roots, stones and similar objects and flower children. During the year different flower children appear according to the changing seasons. Once a certain flower has ceased blooming in nature, its flower child also disappears from the season table. It then reappears as a sleeping root child under a piece of moss or an old root.

Our children often liken these comings and goings on the seasonal tableau with the processes observed in fields and meadows. They look for parallels between what is happening outside and on our season table, and experience and understand that the year is a rhythmically recurring cycle.

We often hear: "Look, the daffodils have come to our seasonal tableau, it must be Easter soon, that's what happened last year." Or one of our children asks: "why are the forget-me-nots flowering outside but not on our season table?"

Every year in late winter and early spring snowdrops tentatively appear, followed by colourful tulips and daffodils, and in summer by daisies and fragrant roses. In autumn we are left with chestnuts, rose-hips and finally Christmas roses as the last messenger of the ending year, until life goes back under the earth and only roots remain, waiting for the right time to show us their miracles again.

The season table shows how nature changes slowly, steadily and in ever recurring rhythms.

In contrast to our daily lives, which are often influenced by the media, advertisements and images geared towards a quick effect, the season table shows the natural rhythm of the earth and its dependability. This gives children, and also adults, support and stability in an apparently ever faster moving world.

The season table should be situated in an easily accessible central part of the house. A quiet place of hardly noticeable change. It invites the onlooker to stand still for a moment, observe and develop their fantasy, leading to inner equilibrium and heightened sense impressions.

The presence of a season table furthers a more observant attitude towards smaller details in life. "What has changed today?" The modern, over-stimulated human being needs to give special attention to develop these kinds of observational abilities.

It is also the place where we as a family get together. Here we tell stories in the evening or sing together before going to bed. It is an essential part of our family life.

The children like to bring back little things from their walks, like snail shells, beautiful moss or autumn fruits to compliment the season table in their own way. Our children understood from an early age not to 'replant' flowers, neither on the season table nor in nature, or to use them as toys.

Visitors who have no experience with the subject and meaning of a season table have the chance to discover and occupy themselves with it and the flower children. Many a beautiful season table has been created after an initial astonished "what have you got there?"

The season table is an image of nature. Just as nature cannot be imagined without flowers, so the flower children belong to the season table. They represent on a small scale the bigger picture of nature.

The seasonal tableaux shown in this book are the result of years of experience. If you are just starting, a simple silk cloth at the corner of your table will suffice as a base. Even a single flower child, a root, some moss, a candle and a bunch of flowers can be seen as a beautiful season table that children still find fascinating.

When our children were small I never changed the season table while they were watching, so that every new stone or feather was welcomed joyfully and with amazement, so it remained mysterious and exciting.

Basic Patterns

The following pages describe the basic patterns for making the different flower children.

The patterns are meant as a guideline for beginners. Once you have mastered the basic forms you will be able to make up your own flower children. All you need are good observational skills in nature and some imagination.

Making the head

It is most important to achieve a smooth head without folds.

Take your time making your first heads. After you have made a few you will have mastered the seemingly difficult processes and they can be made without much effort.

The body size varies from flower child to flower child, and it is mentioned in the instructions for each flower child.

MATERIALS
Wool yarn
Unspun sheep's wool
Thin knitted cotton, 2 3/4 in (7 cm) long, sewn
  into a tube, width depending on head size
Skin-coloured cotton knit, square, 2 3/8 in (6 cm)
  long
Tying off thread

It is important to use soft, stretchy cotton knit for the head. Thick cotton knit will always leave some folds.

The following are the instructions for making a head for a large flower child.

1. Wind a solid ball out of wool yarn remnants, about 3 in (8 cm) in circumference.

2. Gather the cotton knit tube close to the edge at the top end. To do this, sew the thread (always use a double thread) in at the one side and gather round to the other side. Pull the thread tight and sew it in well. Now turn the tube right way out.

3. Place two layers of not too thick unspun sheep's wool in a cross on top of each other, place your yarn ball in the middle of the cross and fold up the ends of the cross (see figure on page 10). Tie up the head right below the yarn ball with strong cotton thread.

4. Put the knitted cotton tube over the wool head, pull it down tightly and tie it right below the yarn ball. To obtain a really round head, roll the head firmly back and forth a few times. Grasp the wool hanging out of the head firmly with one hand, pulling at the cotton knit. If there is now a gap between neck and head, tie up the head again nearer the wool ball, untying the old thread first.

5. Now tie the eye and chin line to form the head. Use a strong, unbreakable thread as it needs to be pulled very tightly. Linen thread or book binding thread are good for this.

For tying up use a knot that is easy to pull tight, but does not come undone by itself.

Beginners can wind the knot over their hand and then slip the loop over the doll's head. To make the knot, lay the thread around the back of your hand. Wind one end around your hand

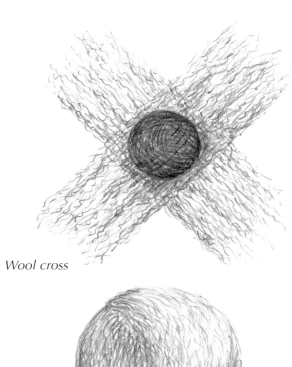

Wool cross

Head tied off, raw form

Tying off eye and chin line

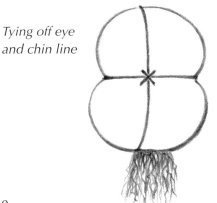

again. Both ends will now be lying along your palm. Put your thumb over one end to hold it tight. The other end is threaded behind your thumb and from below through the lower thread. This end is drawn up again from below through the lower and then the upper thread (see opposite).

Pull on both ends. If you can feel constant pressure around your hand the knot is done correctly. Take the loop off your hand and put around the middle of the doll's head. Pull the knot to make the exact eye line. If it does not work at first, you can easily loosen the knot again by pulling the ends back and forth. If the thread keeps slipping you can fix it at the right height by sticking two pins into the head at the eye line until you have pulled the thread tight. Take out the pins again afterwards. Make sure the eye thread is in the middle of the head. Choose the best side of the head for the face. Pull the thread tight again, tie another knot and push the knot to the ear point. Sew in the threads by passing them right through the head with a long needle, then cut off the ends.

Make the same knot over your hand for the chin line. Lay it vertically over the head, pull it tight and knot it once. Sew a cross over the meeting point of the eye and chin threads at the ear with the thread, then pass the thread through the head and cut off the ends (see figure to left).

6.Now you can form the back of the head. Because the threads have been sewn together at the ear points, the eye line cannot slip anymore and you can pull the thread of the eye line down at the back to the neck. Use a crochet hook for this. Push it under the thread from above and pull the thread down with it to the neck thread.

7. Take your square piece of cotton knit (make sure the rib runs vertically over the head) and lay it over the face to test the face. If the eye line appears too deep, lay a small piece of unspun wool over the thread. You can adjust the depth to your taste. If you cannot see an eye line at all through the cotton knit, then you need to retie it.

If you want to make a small nose (e.g. for gnomes), then sew a few stitches right under the eye line below each other, or even on top of each other. Keep checking what it will look like by stretching the cotton knit over the face.

If you are happy with the face, then stretch the cotton knit over it. The upper edges should not overlap over the top of the head, but the fabric should overlap at the back. Push all the folds at the neck to the back and tie up the head under the chin again. Sew up the back seam making sure the cotton knit is stretched back. To finish, sew up the 'fontanel' on the top of the head.

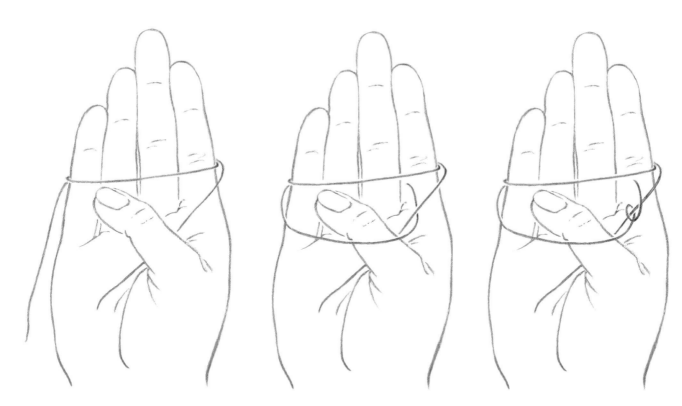

Making a knot for tying up

Making the dress for a flower girl with long skirt

MATERIALS
Craft felt 4 5/8 in x 5 3/4 in (12 cm x 14.5 cm) for the skirt
Craft felt 2 3/8 in x 4 5/8 in (6 cm x 12 cm) for the top

Tips
You do not need to leave a seam allowance for these patterns. Always sew with a double thread. The dress is made out of two pieces, a top with sleeves and a simple skirt as a lower part. The shape of the sleeve depends on the petal of the respective flower children, so it varies from flower child to flower child.

Start with the lower part. Lay the larger square piece of felt down in front of you and fold the longer half up as shown above. This will leave a thin single edge, making it easier to sew the top onto later. Always double the felt for stability. Now fold the felt again lengthways and sew it together with a narrow seam. Sew in the thread, but do not cut off the end. Use the thread to sew a gathering seam around the thin single edge. Let the remaining thread and needle hang down and turn the garment the right way round.

Now sew up the top after cutting the pattern out of the smaller piece of felt. Sew up the sleeve seams and fold the garment in half to cut the neck opening. Do not cut the neck too big. Turn the garment right way out.

Take the head, cut off all the threads hanging down and tease out some of the sheep's wool. Twist this wool tightly together and carefully push it through the top neck opening. The felt will stretch a bit. Pull the top into shape and push the skirt against it from below. Pull the gathering thread tight and sew the thread in at the back (the seam should always be at the centre of the back).

Sew the top and lower part together with mattress stitch so that the seam is invisible.

If the neck opening is too wide, run a gathering thread around it.

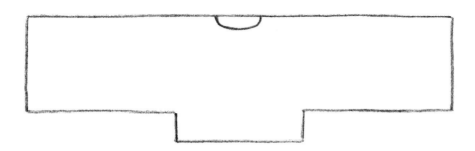

Basic pattern: top, actual size

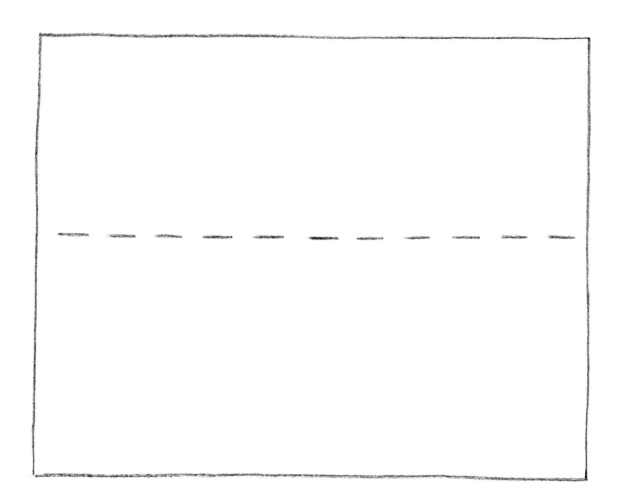

Basic pattern: skirt, actual size

Flower girl with legs

Make the head and body following the instructions for the *Flower boy* (see page 15; head circumference 2 3/4 in (7 cm), arm length 3 1/2–3 7/8 in (9–10 cm), leg length to fit the sewn cotton knit leg).

Wind light-coloured, unspun sheep's wool thinly and evenly around the arms and legs.

Legs

Sew the cotton knit legs according to the pattern. Copy the pattern onto the cotton knit (make sure the rib is running vertically) and cut it out. Fold over the legs lengthways so that the legs are on top of each other. Pin them together and sew with backstitch from the top to the start of the legs. Fold the cotton knit back so you can see two legs again, the cotton knit is double. Sew up along the inside of the leg, sewing a curve at the groin. Turn the right way round and stretch well with a ball-point pen or similar object.

Adjust your pipe-cleaner leg which has been wound with unspun sheep's wool (see page 15) to the length of your cotton knit legs. Bend the feet over about 1/8 in (5 mm) so the sharp pipe-cleaner cannot pierce through the cotton knit. Then pull the cotton knit legs over the pipe-cleaners.

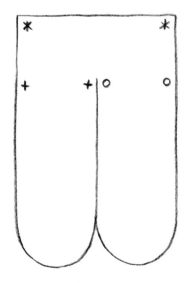

Cotton knit legs, actual size

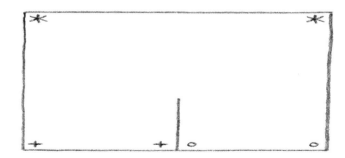

Underpants, actual size

Underpants

Make the underpants out of felt, cotton or silk. Vary the length depending on the flower child and personal preference. Sew the back seam with blanket stitch, then the leg seam. Turn the underpants the right way out and put them on the doll. Depending on pattern and preference, sew a running seam around the base of the underpants' leg.

You can also make the underpants out of a piece of elastic lace. Sew the piece together at the back (measure around the stomach first). Make the legs by sewing the piece together at the groin with a few stitches.

Put the underpants on the doll. Stuff a piece of fluffed unspun sheep's wool into the back to form a bottom. Run a gathering thread around the top of the underpants, pull it tight and sew in the ends of the thread.

Feet

Bend the feet up right angled about 1 in (2.5 cm) with pliers the same as for the flower boy.

Dress

Cut the top of the dress out of felt, cotton or similar fabric. The ends of the sleeves depend on the petals of the flower, and are described in the different flower children patterns.

Sew up the sleeves and side seams of the top.

Make the skirt out of silk, felt or cotton fabric. Make sure the silk has a selvedge to save you hemming it. Cut the skirt out of the fabric according to the instructions for the individual flower children. Run a gathering thread along the top of the skirt and pull it together until it fits the stomach opening of the top. Sew in the threads well and shut the back seam.

Put the top onto to the doll, gather at the neck if necessary, and fasten the hands onto the end of the arms, which should have some unspun sheep's wool wrapped around them.

See if the skirt length is correct and if necessary shorten it. Now sew the skirt to the top with mattress stitch.

Flower boy with legs

Head

Make a head as described above, 2 3/4 in (7 cm) circumference. Shorten the neck to about 1/2 in (1.5 cm). Cut this part right and left (under the ears) until shortly before the tying up the neck thread. Now separate the neck into a front and a back half. These are folded apart.

Body

The body is made out of a frame of pipe-cleaners, over which the clothes are placed.

Take three pipe-cleaners, one for the arms and two for the legs. Bend the leg pipe-cleaners over in the middle and hang them over the arm pipe-cleaner. Twist each leg tightly 2–3 times. Now place the separate neck parts over them and sew first under the arms and then crosswise over the shoulders. Bend the arm pipe-cleaners back to a length of about 3 1/2–3 7/8 in (9–10 cm). The arms should reach just above the head.

Now sew the trousers and put them on. The patterns for the trousers can be found under the instructions for specific flower children. Fold the trousers over so that both legs are on top of each other and sew the back seam to the start of the legs. Sew in the thread and fold the garment so that the seam is in the middle of the back, you will have two legs in front of you. Sew up the inside of the legs. Turn the trousers the right way round and carefully push a ball-point pen or similar object into the legs to make them evenly round.

Only now decide how much to shorten the legs. Take the trousers off again and shorten the legs to the desired length. Do not forget to leave about 1 in (2.5 cm) extra for the foot. Wrap light, unspun sheep's wool around the legs and put the trousers back on. Stuff a piece of fluffy unspun sheep's wool into the back of the trousers to form a bottom. Gather around the top.

Now sew the smock. The patterns can be found in the instructions for the specific flower children.

Sew up the sleeves and side seams. Then turn it right way round and put it on from below. If necessary gather around the neck.

Bend the feet up at right angles about 1 in (2.5 cm) with pliers.

The feet can wear either slippers or boots. Bend them back about 1/8 in (5 mm) at the end to prevent the sharp point of the pipe-cleaner from piercing the slippers or boots.

Shoes

Slippers

Cut the soles out double and glue the two bits together firmly. Sew the top piece on immediately with blanket stitch, as the glue makes the fabric stiff after it has dried. Round out the front and top evenly with a ball-point pen. Fill the front of the slipper with glue and stick it to the foot. If the felt is very difficult to glue then it is artificial felt and might need a few extra stitches to hold everything in place.

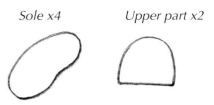

Sole x4   *Upper part x2*

Boots

Wrap some more unspun sheep's wool around the feet. Cut out the soles four times and glue them together as described for the slippers. Now you will need a piece of felt 3 in (8 cm) long and as wide as the boots should be high. Sew the piece starting at the back around the sole with blanket stitch. Cut off any extra felt. Try the boot on and shorten it if necessary. Then sew up the back seam and put it back over the foot. To obtain the form of a boot, fold the excess felt at the front into two folds and sew them up to look like laced boots. Tie a bow at the top.

Sandals

Only make sandals for dolls with legs covered with cotton knit.

Cut the soles out double and glue them together firmly. Sew a band of leather or felt over the foot to the right and left of the sole to make the strap.

Important: Different flower children may have different sized shoes. Because of this, always measure the soles against your doll's foot. The sole of the slipper should stick out a bit at the back of the heel.

Arms

Use a pipe-cleaner for the arms. Buy them from a tobacco shop, as they are stronger than craft pipe-cleaners.

Bend the pipe-cleaner back at the end so that the sharp tip cannot poke through the cotton knit. Push it through the arm opening at the back.

Wind unspun sheep's wool around the bent back end for the hands. Be careful to wrap tightly and without twisting the piece of wool. If the wool tears, just lay the end back down and continue winding. The sheep's wool will stick to itself again.

If you find this method difficult, you can make the winding process easier. Unbend the end of the hand, and wind unspun sheep's wool thinly around it just before and just after the bend. Bend the hand back and wind another piece of unspun sheep's wool thinly around the whole hand. The advantage of this is that the wool will not slip over the bend even if it is not wound tightly enough.

Both hands are made out of a folded piece of cotton knit (see figure, remember fabric grain).

Sew them first and then cut them out. Use a thread colour suited to the cotton knit as one can always see the stitches a bit. Make the hands slightly wider at the base, it makes them easier to turn them the right way round later. Then turn them the right way round, using a ball-point pen or similar object to widen them. Take one of the finished hands, pull it over the wound pipe-cleaner hands and fasten it tightly to the arm at about the elbow by winding the thread around it a few times.

Now pull this arm to its right length. For 'children' the arm should only reach to just above the top of the head. Sew a running thread around the sleeve above the 'petals,' pull it tight around the arm and sew it onto the hand.

Bend the other side of the pipe-cleaner so that it is the same length as the first arm and complete it in the same way. The finished arm length should be about 4 $\frac{5}{8}$ in (12 cm).

Fill the skirt from below with some unspun sheep's wool to finish.

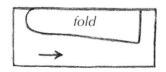

Different hair styles

For the hair styles you can use:
Unspun sheep's wool, long or short staple
Pieces of fur or wool fur fabric
Wool (mohair or bouclé)

Sheep's wool

LONG HAIR WITH FRINGE

To make long hair with a fringe, lay a small strand of wool on the head towards the front. Sew it on with a few stitches. This length of hair is the fringe. For the rest of the hair lay a strand of wool from left to right wide enough to cover the whole head and sew it on with small stitches. If stitches are visible, rub the needle back and forth over the hair so that they disappear under the wool.

You can make braided hair styles out of this long hair, for example plaits or 'monkey swings.'

If you prefer a centre parting for your flower child, lay a small piece of cloth under the centre of the strand of hair wool and sew a straight seam with a sewing machine. Then fasten the strand of hair to the head with a few stitches.

For a shorter hair style use short staple magic wool (unspun sheep's wool), shape it and sew it onto the head with a few stitches. You can usually still make short 'rat tails' or a 'bun' with the ends.

Wig stitched with mohair or bouclé wool

Stitch a cross into the head, and fill in the gaps with further stitches, always guiding the wool under the wool cross. Stitch the fringe slightly irregularly. Then you can carefully brush the hair for a fluffier finish.

Fur or wool fur fabric wig

Tip: Cut wool fur fabric along the cloth under the hair with a sharp pair of scissors to avoid a straight hair line.

Sew the separate triangles together and then put the wig onto the doll. If the wig is too big, correct it at the back. Sew the wig to the head with a few stitches. All the wigs can be made more beautiful by adding a plait or flower head band.

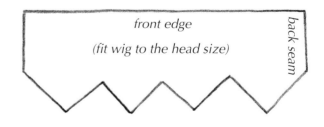

front edge

(fit wig to the head size)

back seam

Making the face

Before you start decorating the doll with a collar, silk dress and petals you can give the doll a personal touch. Although each doll is different despite using the same patterns and clothes, you give it a personal expression when making the face. Because of this, you need to take plenty of time making it. Often your own or your children's faces can be recognised in these faces.

Eyes and mouth

First stick three pins into the face for eyes (two blue pins) and mouth (one red pin). The eyes should always be placed on the eye line and should form an equilateral triangle with the mouth. Careful: eyes that are too close together can appear unfriendly, a mouth that is too high can be mistaken for a nose.

Once you have found the right position you can embroider or draw the eyes and mouth.

EMBROIDERED EYES AND MOUTH

Stitch a suitably coloured double thread from the back of the head, starting with the eyes.

Sew the mouth with a double thread too.

DRAWN EYES AND MOUTH

Carefully pull out the pins and draw small dots in their place with a sharp suitably coloured pencil. Make these dots darker and bigger by pressing the pencil against the cloth until you have the desired size.

You can form the mouth by drawing a line outwards either side of the dot. The line should be straight, not curved up or down. You can make the colour stronger by wetting the pencil.

UNDERLINING THE EYE SOCKETS

Push a needle with a double thread and anchor it firmly under the hair, from the back through the head to the right eye, and push it back into the head 1/32 in (1 mm) further along. Now pull it tight so that it forms a hollow where the eye should be. Repeat for the other eye. You can now either embroider or draw over the eye socket.

Cheeks

Colour a small piece of cotton knit with red and a bit of brown (coloured pencils are good for this) and carefully pat the cheeks with it. Do not worry if the colour has turned out too strong, it will fade after a short time.

Ways to stitch the eyes

Ways to stitch the mouth

Flower stalks

Make the stalks of the flowers that the flower children are holding out of florist's wire or pipe-cleaners wound with green felt. Pipe-cleaners should be 'shaved' evenly with a pair of scissors.

If the flower has a branched stalk (e.g. a forget-me-not) use thin craft wire.

For better stability always double the wire and twist it firmly together. Leave a small wire loop at the top for some flowers (e.g. a snowdrop) on which to hang the dangling blossom.

Wind green doubled sewing thread around very thin stalks. To do this, spread glue around the bottom of the stalk, stick the thread on to it and wind it tightly upwards, gluing the thread to the top of the stalk again. Do not cut the remaining thread off as you can use it to sew the flower onto the stalk.

Thicker stalks can be wound with felt or florist's tape. Florist's tape is only available in a few shades of green, make sure the felt for the leaves is roughly the same colour, otherwise use felt for the stalk.

Florist's tape sticks by itself so it is not necessary to use glue. Lay the tape diagonally along the bottom of the wire and wind it tightly up to the top of the stalk. Press down slight irregularities.

If you want to use felt, cut a long, $1/16$ in (2–3 mm) thin strip of felt. Check the grain of the felt, in one direction it rips very easily. Put glue onto the bottom of the wire and wind diagonally up the stalk, again gluing the felt to the stalk at the top. Tie as tightly and evenly as possible. It is important to use craft glue for all gluing purposes, because it dries clear and cannot be seen afterwards.

Different stitches used

GATHERING STITCH

Gathering or tacking stitch is used for gathering cloth together, as the name suggests. To make a gathering seam push the needle alternately through a piece of cloth and over a piece of cloth.

BACK STITCH

Back stitch is used for sewing two pieces of cloth together without the cloth gathering if the thread is pulled.

To make a back stitch, pick up a few threads of the cloths to be sewn together, then sew a back stitch that exactly meets the end of the last stitch.

BLANKET STITCH

To make a blanket stitch, push the needle from the back to the front and pull the thread through, leaving a small loop. Push the needle through this loop and pull the thread tight.

MATTRESS STITCH

Use mattress stitch for invisible seams. Lay the two cloths beside each other with folded edges together. Push the needle through one cloth from below; now take a small piece of the other cloth and pull tight.

Gathering stitch

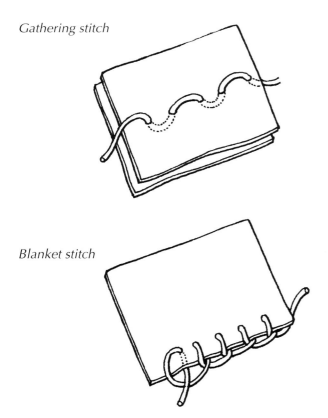

Blanket stitch

Back stitch

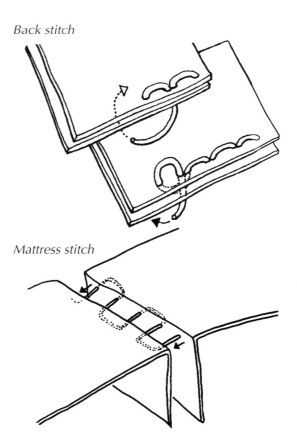

Mattress stitch

21

Spring

Spring is a fascinating time for children. They can spend more time outside; new life is all around them. Small green shoots push up from under the ground, quickly turning into leaves and flowers. Thick buds on the trees — visibly waiting in winter — burst into bloom. All around it is green and flowering. The birds have arrived back from their winter habitats and welcome us with joyful song. Everywhere you look you can find young animals.

Even if there are still few flower children on the seasonal tableau your children will soon gather anything interesting they find in nature to bring it to life.

Butterflies

MATERIALS
Coloured magic wool
Black craft pipe-cleaners

For a large butterfly, cut a 6 ¹/₄ in (16 cm) long stretch of pipe-cleaner and fold it in half in the middle.

Tease a square out of magic wool. You can lay a few thin strands of another colour on top. Put the wool into the folded pipe-cleaner and push the pipe-cleaner together in the middle. Twist the ends of the pipe-cleaner together twice and pull the ends apart to make the feelers.

If the magic wool looks a bit disorderly, 'knead' it into shape or twist the lower wings into a tip.

Butterfly child

MATERIALS
Black velour for the body and hat
Black magic wool for hair

Coloured magic wool for the wings
Black felt for the feelers

Make a head, 2 in (5 cm) in circumference. Only tie off the eye line.

Make hands and body the same as for the *Bee child* (page 41), but do not gather around the waist.

Use a 2 ³/₄ in (7 cm) long craft pipe-cleaner for the wings. Fold the two ends a quarter of the way inwards, you now have a double pipe-cleaner half the length. Tease a square of magic wool for the wings (as described for the butterfly), with a few strands of another colour placed on top if you wish. Lay the wool in the folded pipe-cleaner and push the pipe-cleaner together in the middle. Fasten the wings to the body by sewing the black pipe-cleaner directly to the body under the head. Cut the feelers out of black felt and sew them to the left and right of the head.

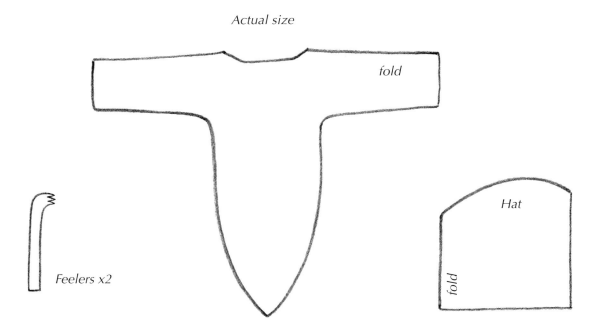

Actual size

fold

Feelers x2

Hat

fold

Flowers and blossoms

MATERIALS
Different coloured strands of wool

Lay six small strands of wool together. Use a different colour for the centre of the flower and group the other five colours in a bundle around the centre colour. Tie them all together with thread about 3/7 in (1 cm) from the top.

Now cut the hanging down pieces of magic wool just below the thread.

Magic wool ducks

MATERIALS
Short staple yellow magic wool
Some red magic wool

Wind a thin strand of yellow wool around your finger 4 or 5 times. Take the wool off your finger and sew it together with a few stitches. Wind a small loose ball for the head out of yellow wool and sew it onto the body. Sew on a fluff of red wool for the beak, twisting it to make a point at the front.

Caterpillar

MATERIALS
Strand of wool
Wool remnants

Make a knot in the middle of a 7 1/2 in (20 cm) long strand of magic wool or unspun sheep's wool. Place the upper half of the wool over the knot and spread it evenly around the knot. Tie off the ball you have now made with a thin strand of wool. This ball is the head of the caterpillar. If you find it hard to tie off with a strand of wool you can also use thread.

Wind five small balls (1 1/4 in (3 cm) diameter) with wool remnants for the different sections. Place the first ball behind the head, spread the strand of wool evenly around the ball and tie off right behind the ball. Follow the same procedure for the other four balls.

Cut of the strand of wool behind the last ball. Push a short strand of magic wool through the head for feelers.

Strawberry children

Strawberry girl

MATERIALS
Make the basic form for the dress and body as for the *Flower girl with long skirt.*
Red felt for the dress
Green felt for the jacket

Make the body and dress according to the instructions for the *Flower girl with long skirt,* head circumference 3 in (8 cm). Make the dress out of red felt.

Cut the jacket out of green felt. Use the same pattern as for the upper part of the dress. Sew this top onto the arms with buttonhole stitch, but do not turn inside out. The arms are slightly wider because of this and can easily be pulled over the red sleeves. Cut the sleeves into points at the wrists in imitation of real strawberry leaves. Cut the jacket open in the middle. Measure the circumference of the bottom of the jacket and cut a strip of felt edging the same length following the pattern for the collar of the strawberry boy. Sew it wrong side to wrong side to the jacket and then pull it downwards. Put the jacket on and sew it together at the top at the front with a small bead.

Strawberry boy

MATERIALS
See *Flower boy with legs*
Red felt for clothes and hat
Green felt for collar and boots

Make the body according to the instructions for *Flower boy with legs,* head circumference 2 3/4 in (7 cm). For smock and trousers use the pattern for the *Grass child* (page 36).

Cut the hat out of red felt, fold it, sew it together and turn it right side out. Embroider small green stitches on the hat (strawberry seeds), using a green double sewing thread.

Cut the collar out of green felt with strawberry leaf edging. Cut irregular points into the edge. If you find it difficult cutting points you can also use pinking shears. Fasten the collar with a few stitches to the back of the smock.

Make green felt boots for the feet.

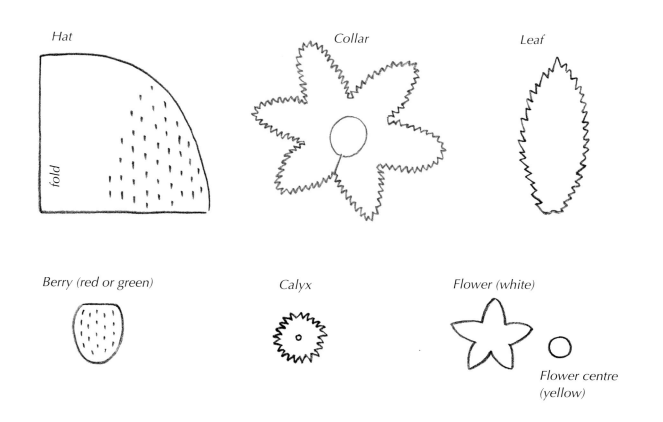

Hat

fold

Collar

Leaf

Berry (red or green)

Calyx

Flower (white)

Flower centre (yellow)

Blossom

MATERIALS
Green, red, white and yellow felt
Craft wire, 5 $1/2$ in (14 cm) and 3 $7/8$ in (10 cm)
Green sewing thread

First cut the two strawberry pieces out of red felt. Sew them together, leaving a small opening at the top, and carefully turn right side out. Stuff the berry with some fluffy unspun sheep's wool and embroider small green dots over it for the 'strawberry seeds.' Shut the top opening and sew one of the two green felt calyx to the top. If you want to add an unripe fruit, cut a smaller berry out of light green felt and follow the instructions described above.

Now cut out the white flower and the yellow flower centre and glue the flower centre to the middle of the white flower. Sew a few white threads into the yellow centre for pistils and colour them red with a pencil. Stick the calyx to the back of the flower.

To make the stalk, twist the wire together tightly. Leave a small loop at the top on which to fasten the berry or the flower. Depending on how many strawberries you want to hang from them you will need two or three such stalks. Place all the wires together without twisting them and wind green thread around them, starting from the base. Make sure the loops are at the top of the stalk. Once the stalk is finished, sew the flower and berry/berries through the loop onto the calyx. Now cut the leaves out of green felt and fasten them to the lower end of the stalk.

The strawberries can be enlarged and given to the flower girl to hold without a stalk.

Dandelion child

MATERIALS
See *Flower boy with legs*
Craft pipe-cleaners for the legs
Green felt
Light yellow felt 1 in x 11 $^3/_4$ in (2.5 cm x 30 cm)
Dark yellow felt 1 in x 3 in (2.5 cm x 8 cm)
Pipe-cleaners for the stalk
White magic wool for the dandelion puff-ball
   hair

Flower child

Make the body according to the instructions for *Flower boy with legs,* head circumference 3 in (8 cm).

Use craft pipe-cleaners for this flower child as its legs are slightly longer than the others described in the basic pattern. Follow the basic pattern and shorten the legs only after putting on the trousers. Cut a V-neck into the smock and glue a piece of light knitted cloth behind the opening. Gather the top opening of the felt smock to make the knitted cloth more visible.

Make a small white ball out of magic wool for the hair and then push it apart in the middle to make an oval. Glue this part to the head. The finished hair should look like a dandelion puff-ball. Brown felt boots are the finishing touch for this flower child.

Flower and stalk

Wind green felt around the 3 $^1/_2$ in (9 cm) long pipe-cleaner.

Roll the dark yellow strip of felt completely around the top of the stalk and fasten it tightly at its base. Now wind the light yellow felt around this cylinder and also fasten it well at the base. Sew in the thread by pushing the needle right

through the felt cylinder a few times. Cut the calyx out of green felt and push it up the stalk to the yellow felt flower. If you have not wound the flower tightly enough you might have to enlarge the calyx. Gather the top of the calyx and sew it around the flower. Sew the thread in at the base of the calyx to the stalk.

Now cut into the flower. Use a small, pointed pair of sharp scissors. Cut the rolled felt in layers from the outside to the inside by cutting $^3/_{16}$ in (0.5 cm) wide strips right down to the green calyx. Glue two of the yellow strips together at the top over the visible piece of pipe-cleaner.

Sew the green felt leaf to the base of the stalk. First glue a 'shaved' green pipe-cleaner to the middle of the underside of the leaf as a central vein. This also gives the leaf more stability.

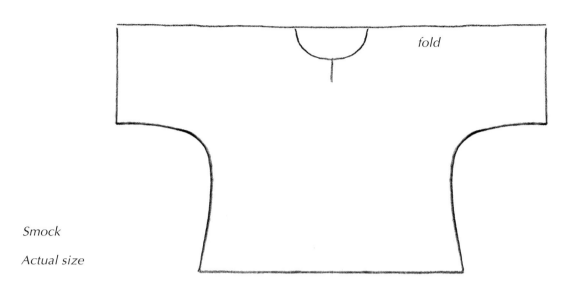

fold

Smock

Actual size

Trousers

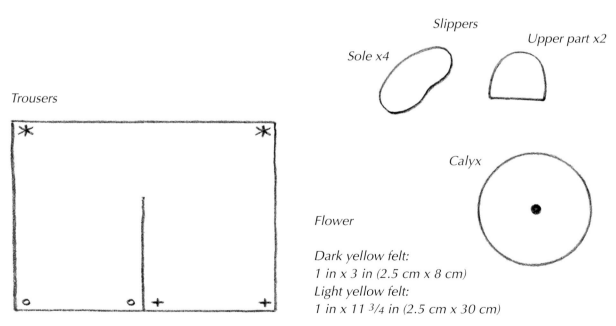

Slippers

Sole x4

Upper part x2

Calyx

Flower

Dark yellow felt:
1 in x 3 in (2.5 cm x 8 cm)
Light yellow felt:
1 in x 11 3/4 in (2.5 cm x 30 cm)

30

Dandelion leaves

Daisy child

MATERIALS
White felt for the flower petals and collar
Green felt for the dress and the leaf
Yellow felt for the flower centre
Florist's tape or green felt for winding around the
    stalk
Cardboard

Flower child

Make the body according to the basic pattern for
Flower girl with long skirt, head circumference
2 ³/₈ in (6 cm). The pattern for the dress is
opposite.

Cut the collar out of white felt, fit it to your
flower child and sew it to the back with a few
stitches. Only now cut in the flower petals, otherwise the collar will stretch too much.

Flowers and stalks

Cut the centre of the flower out of yellow felt and
cardboard. Stick the two pieces together and cut
into the overhanging felt at regular intervals so
you can fold it over and glue it to the back of the
cardboard.

Wind green felt or florist's tape around the two
florist's wires while the centre is drying. Do not
forget to first bend the wire over in the middle
and twist the ends together.

Now cut the flowers and calyx and push them
onto the stalks. Carefully pierce a hole into the
cardboard centre (but not into the felt) with a pair
of sharp scissors. Stick the top end of the stalk
into this hole. Now stick the flower against the
flower centre before cutting the petals. Once this
has dried a bit, stick the calyx from below in a

conical shape and fasten it to the flower and stalk
with a few stitches. You can redden the flower
slightly with a red pencil either underneath or on
top. Now you can cut the petals. To finish, cut a
few leaves out of green felt and sew them to the
stalks at the base.

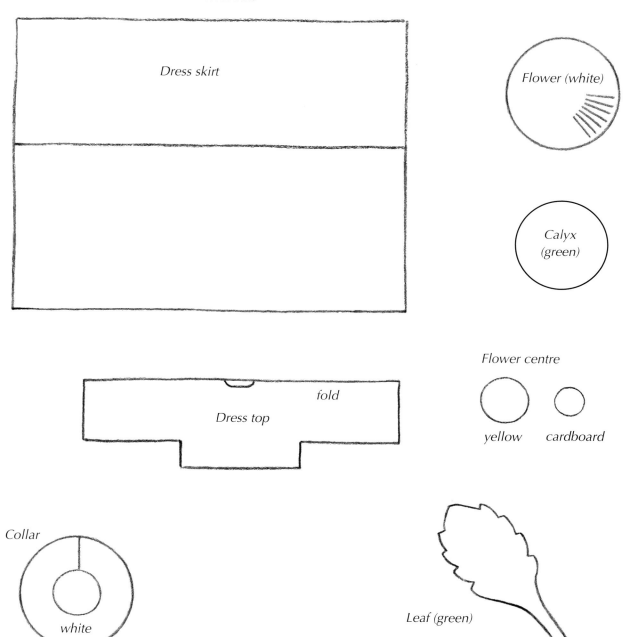

Actual size

Dress skirt

Flower (white)

Calyx
(green)

fold

Dress top

Flower centre

yellow   cardboard

Collar

white

Leaf (green)

33

Daffodil child

MATERIALS

For making the body and dress, see the basic pattern instructions for *Flower girl with long skirt.*

Yellow felt for dress and flowers

Florist's wire and pipe-cleaners for the stalk

Florist's tape or green felt for winding around the stalk

Green felt for the leaves and jacket

Yellow magic wool

Flower child

Make the body and dress according to the instructions for the *Flower girl with long skirt,* head circumference 3 in (8 cm).

Use the sleeve ending shown in the figure opposite.

Cut the jacket out of green felt and fit it to the flower child. Sew on a yellow bead for a button.

Flower and stalk

Cut the flower and the flower calyx out of yellow felt. Cut points into the flower calyx, narrowly sew the edges together and turn right side out. Gather the narrow end to fit it to the inner circle (opposite) of the flower. If you draw the circle with a magic marker, where the lines disappear after a short time, you can sew the flower calyx to the circle with small mattress stitches. If you do not have one of those, you can sew the circle with temporary stitches first. Once the flower calyx is sewn on, carefully cut these stitches from the back and remove the threads.

Wind green felt or florist's tape around the 'shaved' pipe-cleaner. Wind light brown felt around the top 1 1/4 in (3 cm) of the upper end. Cut a small hole into the centre of the flower and

push the pipe-cleaner through this hole about 3/8 in (1 cm). Sew it to the flower with small stitches. Stick a small fluffy piece of magic wool into the calyx. Bend the flower down at the brown part of the stalk.

Cut the leaves twice out of green felt following the pattern. Glue the pieces together with a length of florist's wire between them so that the leaf can be bent down without hanging limply. The wire should end just before the end of the leaf so it remains invisible. Sew the end of the leaf around the stalk with small stitches. Now bend the leaf downwards.

Jacket (green)

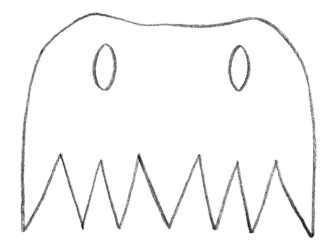

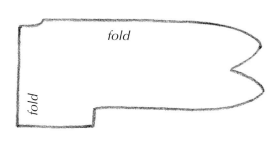

fold

fold

Flower

do not cut
out

Calyx

Leaf

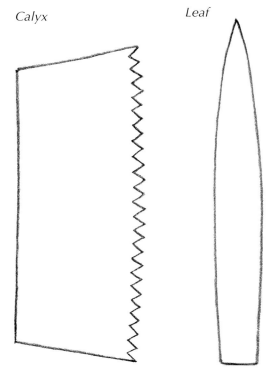

Grass child

MATERIALS
See *Flower boy with legs*
Green felt for clothes and smock
A blade of grass
Small wooden bead

Make the body, trousers and smock according to the instructions for *Flower boy with legs*, head circumference 2 3/4 in (7 cm).

Cut the cape out of green felt. Sew up the top of the hood, turn the cape and gather it around the neck. Fit it to the flower boy and pull the neck to the desired width. Leave a small gap. The cape should not overlap at the front. Fasten the cape to the doll's left and right shoulders with a few stitches. Sew a wooden bead to one side of the cape for a button.

Cut slits for the arms into the side of the cape. You can enlarge them to incorporate the arms' gesture.

Make slippers out of green felt for the feet.

Cape

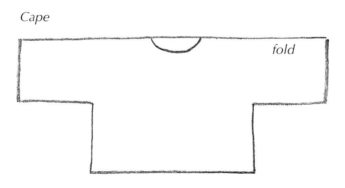

fold

Actual size

Smock

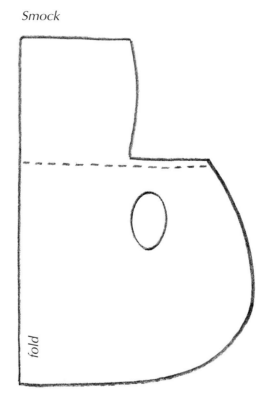

fold

Trousers

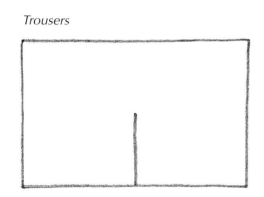

37

Forget-me-not child

MATERIALS

Make the body and dress according to the instructions for the *Flower girl with long skirt.*

Blue felt for dress and flowers

Florist's wire and thin craft wire for the stalk

Florist's tape or green felt for winding around the stalk

Green felt for the leaves

Purple felt for the buds

Flower child

Make the body and dress according to the instructions for Flower girl with long skirt, head circumference 3 in (8 cm).

Use the same pattern for the petal-edging around the sleeves and for the strip of felt around the stomach.

Gather the stomach strip of petals to the length of the top of the dress, pull it tight and fasten it to the dress with a few stitches.

Flowers and stalk

Cut a piece of wire 7 $^3/4$ in (20 cm) long for the stalk. Bend this wire in half and twist the ends together. Make 3–4 twigs along the stalk by twisting a thin double craft wire together and winding it around the stalk 2–3 times. Make sure you twist it tightly, if necessary use a pair of pliers. Now wind florist's tape or felt around the stalk. You might need to start anew for each branch, in which case the felt or florist's tape should overlap slightly.

Next cut out the flowers. Sew 3–4 stitches into the centre with yellow thread and use this thread

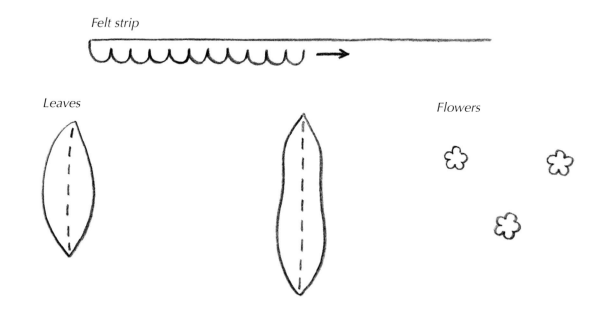

Felt strip

Leaves

Flowers

for sewing the flower to the stalk. You can use this thread for the other flowers by pushing the needle under the felt or florist's tape to the next flower. Sew as many flowers to the stalks as you like.

You can fasten small purple buds to the ends of the twig by cutting out small pieces of purple felt $1/16$ in x $1/32$ in (2 x 1 mm) and, using a lot of glue, twisting them around the tip of the twig, moulding and if necessary cutting them into shape.

Cut the leaves (2–3) out of green felt. Using back stitch, sew a decorative seam along the middle of the leaf from top to bottom. Fasten the leaves to the middle of the stalks.

Make the flower wreath for the head by sewing one flower to the head, then pushing the needle under the hair to the next flower and sewing it on, etc.

Summer

Summer starts around the 21st of June with the longest day and shortest night of the year. Children experience this with all their senses. They can feel the sun's warmth on their bare skin, smell fragrant hay, watch clouds moving overhead, build sand-castles and harvest delicious berries. Caring for the flowers that bloom all around is fun even for very small children. Nature is so fascinating that children look upon her with awe.

Bee child

MATERIALS
Striped velour for the body
Black velour for the hat
Black magic wool for the hair
Black felt for the feelers
Pipe-cleaners for the arms
Yellow raffia for the wings

Make a head 2 in (5 cm) in circumference. Only tie off the eye line. The basic structure of the arms is a pipe-cleaner, length about 3 1/2 in (9 cm). Shorten the arms to their correct length once the bee child has received its dress. To fasten the arms to the head, cut the neck nearly up to the tying off thread at the sides right and left (the same as for *Flower boy with legs)*, push in the arm pipe-cleaner and wind the tying off thread around the pipe-cleaner and neck.

Now cut the body out of striped velour, sew it together and turn it the right way out. Stuff some unspun sheep's wool into the base and fit it to the bee child. Gather the neck at the same time as sewing the raw edge inwards to prevent the velour unravelling.

Shorten the arms to the right length and wind some unspun sheep's wool around the hands. Make the hands out of a circular piece of cotton knit. Pull them tightly over the pipe-cleaner arms and tie them off tightly with a double thread. Push the rest of the cotton knit into the sleeves with a pair of small sharp scissors. Gather the arms, turning in the raw edge and sewing it the same as for the neck, pull the gathering thread tight and sew them to the wrists.

Gather the body under the arms with a black thread to make the bee child's waist. Pull in the gathering thread and sew it in.

41

Cut the hat out of black velour. Sew the curve at the top together and turn it right way round. Gather the hat at the base, making it fit from ear to ear. Sew the hat to the edge of the body at the neck by laying both right sides of the velour together and sewing them together; that is, sew the hat with the inside towards the body. Put black magic wool onto the head for hair and pull the hood over the head. Fasten it to the forehead with a few stitches. Cut the feelers out of black felt and sew them to the right and left of the head.

Make the wings out of raffia. Flatten it to cut the pattern out. Fasten these wings to the right and left underneath the hat by pinching the end of the two wings together (do not gather with a needle as the raffia will tear) and sewing each one on with a few stitches.

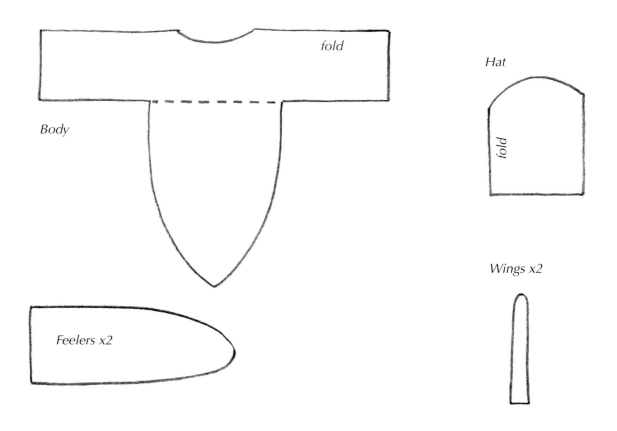

fold

Hat

Body

fold

Wings x2

Feelers x2

Wild rose child

MATERIALS

See basic pattern for the *Flower girl with long skirt* for the skirt and dress.

Pink felt for dress and flowers

White silk for the petal dress

Thin wire and pipe-cleaner for the stalk

Florist's tape or green felt for winding around the stalk

Green felt for the leaves and collar

Yellow felt

Yellow sewing silk

Flower child

Make the body according to the instructions for *Flower girl with long skirt.* Use the following pattern for the sleeve ending. The head circumference is 3 in (8 cm).

Make the dress out of pink felt.

Cut the petal dress out of silk with a good sharp pair of scissors. If it is too long for your flower girl, shorten it at the upper edge. Gather this edge close to the top. Make sure two of the petals are hanging at the front and the other two at the back. Sew the dress up at one shoulder with 2 or 3 stitches. Cut the collar out of green felt and fasten it over the silk dress. Finish by pulling the open blade of a wide pair of scissors over the silk dress from top to bottom to make the petals curl outwards.

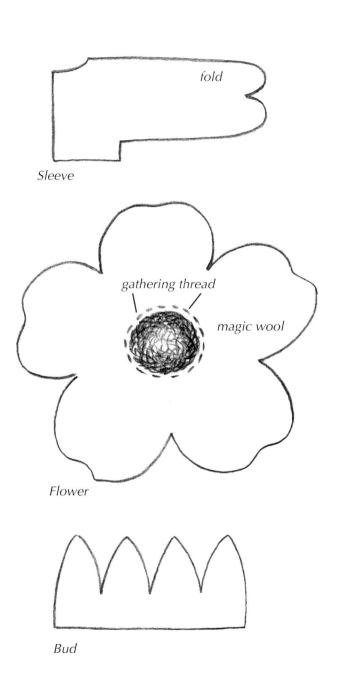

fold

Sleeve

gathering thread

magic wool

Flower

Bud

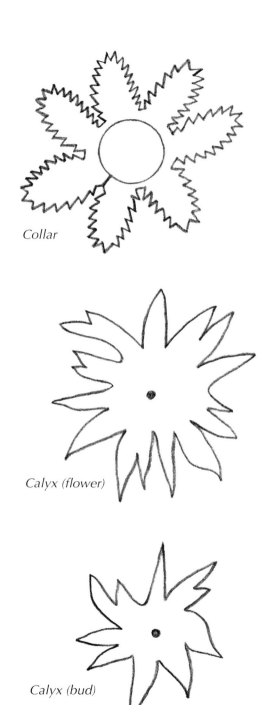

Collar

Calyx (flower)

Calyx (bud)

44

Flower and stalk

Shave a 5 $\frac{1}{2}$ in (14 cm) long pipe-cleaner and lay a 5 $\frac{1}{2}$ in (14 cm) thin wire beside it. Wind florist's tape or felt around both for 2 $\frac{3}{4}$ in (7 cm), then wind them separately. Cut the calyx out of green felt and push it onto the wound pipe-cleaner. Then push the flower over it. Push them up to the top of the pipe-cleaner and put some yellow magic wool over the end. Form the magic wool into a circle by sewing back and forth, over a circumference of $\frac{3}{8}$ in (1 cm). Fasten the flower to the stalk while sewing this centre. Once the magic wool has turned into a round flat form, make the stamen by sewing tiny loops over the whole flower centre with yellow sewing silk. Cut the loops open and shorten all the threads to the same length.

Gather the calyx about $\frac{3}{8}$ in (1 cm) from its centre and push it up just below the flower. Pull the gathering thread tightly, there should now be a slight thickening of the lower end of the calyx.

Sew the thread in by sewing through the stalk a few times, then lightly glue the edge of the calyx to the rose petals. Finish by gathering around the centre of the flower and pulling in the thread to slightly gather the flower petals.

Cut the bud out of pink felt. First push the calyx onto the wound wire stalk. Now glue the felt strip of petals around the stalk and sew the end in with a stitch.

Push the calyx right up to the bud and gather it below the petals. Pull the thread tightly and sew it in well, which will make the base thicker. Stick the innermost two petals lightly together.

If you do not like felt for the bud, you can also use suitably coloured starched silk.

To make this, spray starch (the kind used for starching shirts) onto the silk and iron it, following the instructions on the packet, before cutting it out. This makes the silk stronger and stops the petals from hanging down.

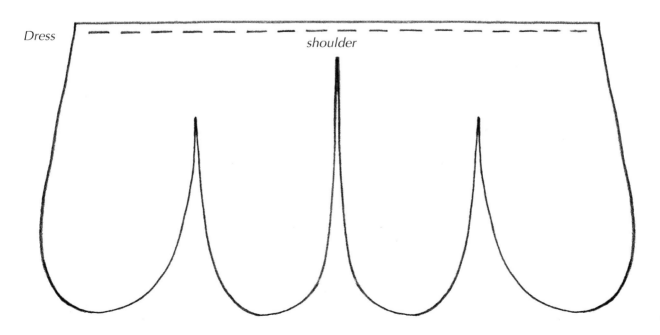

Dress   shoulder

45

Marguerite child

MATERIALS
See basic pattern for *Flower girl with legs*
White silk for the dress
White felt
Green felt for jacket and leaves
Yellow felt for the flower centre
Pipe-cleaner for the stalk
Florist's tape or green felt for winding around the stalk
Cardboard
Some unspun sheep's wool

Flower child

Make the body and dress according to the instructions for *Flower girl with legs,* head circumference 2 3/4 in (7 cm). Use the following pattern for the sleeve endings.

Cut the jacket out of green felt and fasten it under the arms with two or three stitches.

Flower and stalk

Wind florist's tape or green felt around a 4 5/8 in (12 cm) long pipe-cleaner.

Cut out a cardboard circle and pierce a small hole in the centre for the stalk. Glue a small fluff of magic wool to the cardboard. The wool should not reach beyond the edges of the cardboard. Then cut a circle out of yellow felt and cover the cardboard with it. Glue the felt to the magic wool, cut into the overhanging edge every 3/16 in (0.5 cm) and glue this edge to the back of the cardboard. Make sure the felt fits tightly over the edges of the cardboard circle. Glue the wound pipe-cleaner stalk to the cardboard from below.

Now cut out the white felt circle for the flower. Push this up the stalk and stick it to the back of

the flower centre's felt circle. Only now cut the flower petals into the white felt circle. Finish by pushing the fringed calyx up the stalk and gluing it to the back of the flower. Roughen the surface of the yellow flower centre with a needle. Carefully pull and push the flower petals over and under each other to give the flower its typical slightly irregular look. Now cut two leaves out of green felt and fasten them individually, and in a staggered pattern, to the stalk with a few stitches.

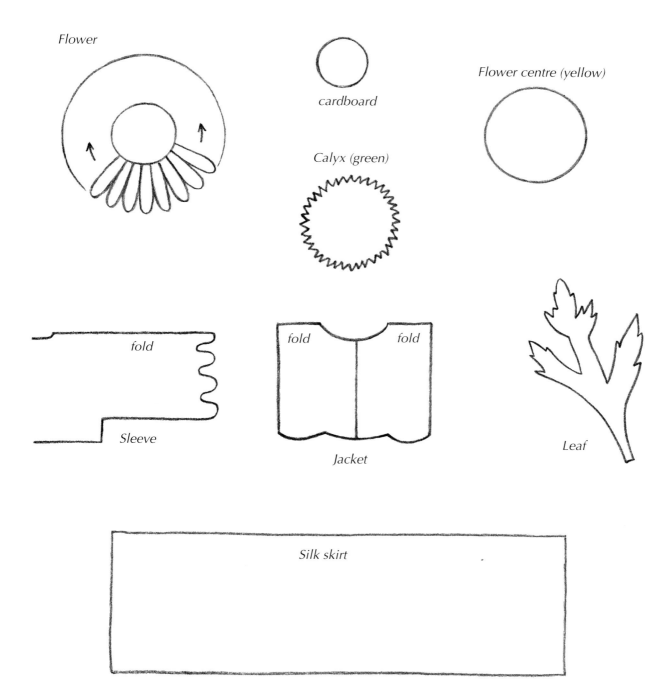

Flower

cardboard

Flower centre (yellow)

Calyx (green)

fold

Sleeve

fold   fold

Jacket

Leaf

Silk skirt

Sunflower child

MATERIALS
For the body and dress, see instructions for the basic pattern for *Flower girl with long skirt.*
Yellow felt for dress and flower petals
Dark brown felt for the jacket
2 pipe-cleaners for the stalk
Florist's tape or green felt for winding around the stalk
Green felt for the leaves
Small black glass beads
Cardboard
Unspun sheep's wool

Flower child

Make the body and dress according to the instructions for *Flower girl with long skirt,* head circumference 3 in (8 cm) Use the following pattern for the sleeve endings.

Cut the jacket out of dark brown felt and put it on the doll.

Flower and stalk

Cut a circle out of cardboard for the flower centre and glue on some unspun sheep's wool. Then cut out the dark brown felt circle and stick it over the cardboard by gluing it to the unspun sheep's wool, cutting into the overhanging edge every 3/16 in (0.5 cm) and gluing it well to the back of the cardboard. Make sure that the felt is pulled tightly over the cardboard circle's edges.

Now cut the flower petals out of yellow felt and glue them side by side to the back of the flower centre. The petals should only slightly overlap the brown felt at the back, you should still be able to see the cardboard. Glue the second round of flower petals staggered behind the first row.

Lay two pipe-cleaners beside each other for the stalk and wind florist's tape or green felt around them both. Place this stalk over the back of the flower centre and glue it to the cardboard. Let it dry slightly before proceeding.

In the meantime, cut the calyx and serated leaf out of green felt. Stitch veins onto the leaf.

Glue the strip of calyx to the back of the flower centre, starting at the outside and spiralling inwards. Glue it over the stalk. The circle should not be bigger than the circumference of the flower centre. Let the glue dry a bit again before sewing the leaves to the lower end of the stalk. Sew the lower, long end of the leaf right around the stalk.

To finish, spread glue over the dark brown flower centre and cover it with small black glass beads. To do this, empty the beads onto a small plate and press the flower centre down onto them. Let the flower dry for some hours and then pull the petals slightly forward.

Because this flower is heavier than the other flowers, you might have to try out different positions before the flower child is able to stand and hold it without falling over.

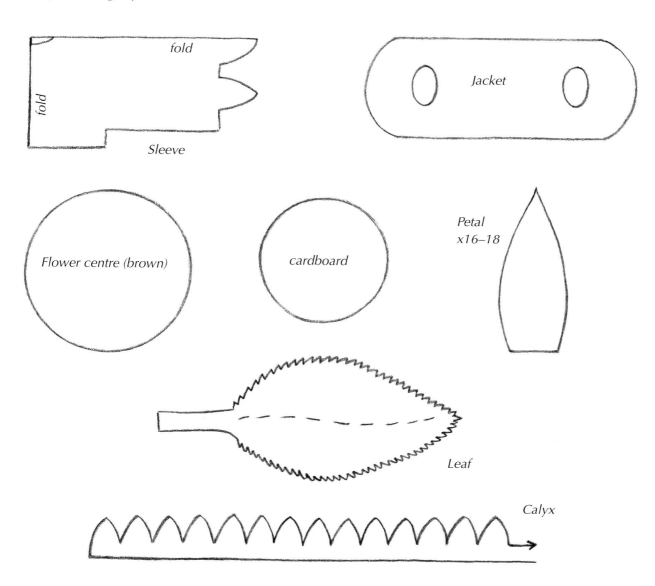

fold

fold

Sleeve

Jacket

Flower centre (brown)

cardboard

Petal x16–18

Leaf

Calyx

Rose child

MATERIALS

For body and dress, see basic instructions for *Flower girl with long skirt.*
White felt for the dress
White silk for the petal dress
Florist's wire and pipe-cleaner for the stalk
Florist's tape or green felt for winding around the stalk
Green felt for the leaves and the collar

Flower child

Make the body according to the instructions for *Flower child with long skirt,* head circumference 3 in (8 cm).

Make the dress out of white felt and the petal dress out of white silk. Make the dress and petal dress as described for *Wild rose child* (page 43).

Flower and stalk

You will need a strip of white silk 2 3/4 in x 17 1/2 in (7 cm x 45 cm) long for the flower.

Fold this strip in half and strengthen the centre fold by going over it with a ruler a few times. You now have a 1 3/8 in (3.5 cm) wide strip. Wind a solid tube out of the first 2–3 cm and fasten it with a few stitches. Then repeatedly make small folds around the tube and sew them tight. To finish, sew in the thread and wind it around the base a few times. Cut five rose petals out of white silk. Gather the first petal and sew it to the flower. Then gather the second petal and sew it slightly overlapping the first petal. Proceed in the same fashion with the other three petals. To finish, wind the thread around the base again a few times.

Make the stalk out of a 4 5/8 in (12 cm) long

pipe-cleaner. Wind florist's tape or green felt around it and fasten a small twig, made from florist's wire, for the rose bud, about two thirds of the way up. Wind green felt or florist's tape around this piece.

Cut the calyx out of green felt. Before fastening it to the stalk, wind unspun sheep's wool around the stalk and twig about 3/4 in (2 cm) from the top to make it thicker. Wind florist's tape or green felt around it. Push the larger calyx and then the flower from the top onto the stalk and glue them tight. Fold the calyx petals upwards and glue them around the bottom of the flower petals.

Push the calyx for the rose bud onto the twig. To make the bud, use a 1 1/2 in x 2 in (4 cm x 5 cm) piece of white silk, fold it in half as for the rose flower so that it is 3/4 in (2 cm) wide. Wind the silk tightly around the upper end of the twig, covering it in glue beforehand. Now glue the calyx tightly to the bud, and glue the top of the bud together.

Make a cross out of wire for the branched leaves, one wire 3 1/2 in (9 cm) long, the other 1 1/4 in (3 cm). Fold the 1 1/4 in (3 cm) wire 1/2 in (1.5 cm) from the top around the 3 1/2 in (9 cm) wire so that three parts of the cross are 1/2 in (1.5 cm) long. Wind florist's tape or green felt around the cross. Cut the leaves out of green felt, cutting the pointed edge of the leaf with a small pair of scissors. Embroider a central vein down the middle of each leaf from top to bottom. Fasten the leaves to the three short ends of the cross, overlapping by 3/8 in (1 cm).

Place the leaf stalk onto the lower end of the flower stalk and wind around them both tightly.

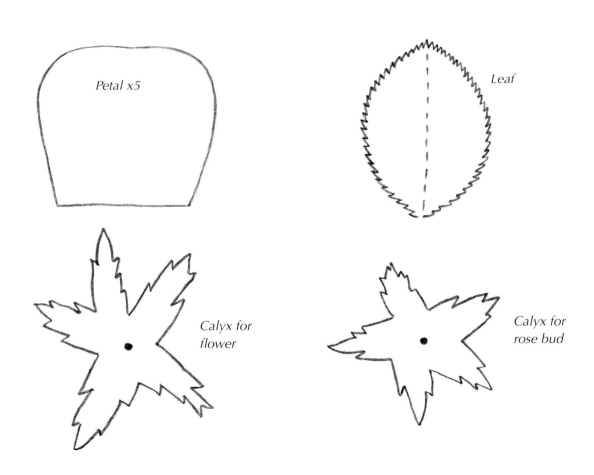

Petal x5

Leaf

Calyx for flower

Calyx for rose bud

Ivy child

MATERIALS
See basic pattern for *Flower boy with legs*
Green felt
7 3/4 in (20 cm) florist's wire for the stalk
7 x 2 in (5 cm) long florist's wire for the twigs

Flower child

Make the body according to the instructions for *Flower boy with legs*, head circumference 2 3/4 in (7 cm).

Make the clothes for the ivy boy out of green felt, using the *Grass child* pattern (page 36), with green felt slippers for its feet.

Ivy tendril

Make the main stalk of the ivy tendril with a piece of single florist's wire. Do not twist the different stalks together but place them beside each other and wind florist's tape or green felt around both of them for 3/8 in (1 cm). Fasten the leaf stalks randomly onto the main stalk and only bend the tendril into shape when you have finished.

Now cut out the leaves. The top three leaves are the smaller ones. Embroider the veins onto the leaves with green thread (see pattern below). Fasten one leaf to each leaf stalk. To do this, overlap the leaf and stalk 3/16 in (0.5 cm) and sew the leaf on with buttonhole stitch.

Leaves

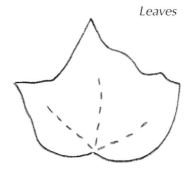

Different children

Make the body according to the instructions for *Flower girl with legs,* head circumference 2 3/4 in (7 cm).

The children's clothes can also be knitted or crocheted.

1. Child with cherry basket

MATERIALS
Edging or cloth for the dress
Cotton, cotton knit or felt for the top
Elastic thread
Red wooden beads
Florist's wire
Small basket

DRESS
Make the dress out of a piece of edging to save hemming. If you want to make it out of fabric, add a seam allowance.

Sew small, close buttonhole stitches around the edge of the sleeve. Fold the three upper parts of the dress over and sew a seam along the back to make a tube. Before putting the dress onto the doll, sew a shirt out of cotton, cotton knit or felt. Use the pattern for *Flower girl with long skirt.* If you sew a cotton top, cut the back open, as cotton does not stretch and you will not be able to put it on otherwise. Sew this opening up after dressing the doll. Then put on the dress and gather the top through the tube with elastic

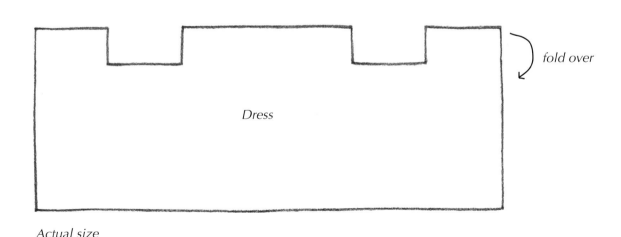

fold over

Dress

Actual size

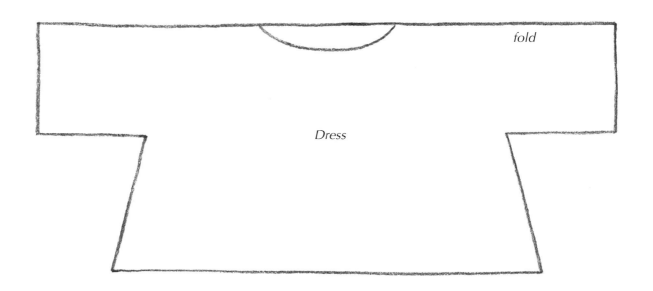

fold

Dress

Actual size

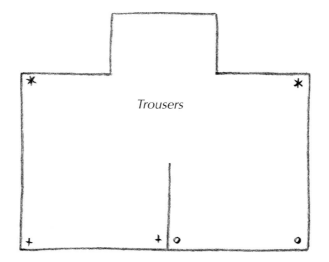

Trousers

54

thread or embroidery thread. You can also cut the embroidery thread or elastic thread at the arms and tie a ribbon for decoration. Knot the thread and sew in the ends. Sew up the back of the dress with mattress stitch.

CHERRIES

Cut a piece of florist's wire 1 1/4 in (3 cm) long and bend back the end. Push a red wooden bead onto every bent back end, making sure it fits tightly. If necessary, use glue as well.

Girl

MATERIALS
Thin cotton fabric for the dress

Make the dress out of a piece of thin cotton. If the fabric does not have a selvedge, add seam allowance. Sew the side and sleeve seams together, flatten them and turn the garment the right way out. Put the dress on the doll and then gather the neck, hemming the top edge at the same time. Do the same for the sleeves. To make the head wreath, twist small fluffs of unspun sheep's wool into tiny balls and sew them around the head. Leave the thread visible between each wool ball.

Boy

MATERIALS
Checked cotton fabric for the shirt
Felt for the trousers and straps
2 small wooden beads

Cut the shirt out of the checked fabric and sew it together as described for the girl above. Cut the trousers out of felt and sew them together. To make a turned up edge, fold the trouser leg end up inside before sewing, then if necessary sew the turned up edge tight with two stitches after turning the trousers right way round. Cut two thin strips of felt for the straps and sew them to the back of the trousers. Now put the trousers on, cross the straps at the back and sew them to the front of the trousers. Sew two wooden beads for buttons to the front. Glue pockets to the trousers if you wish.

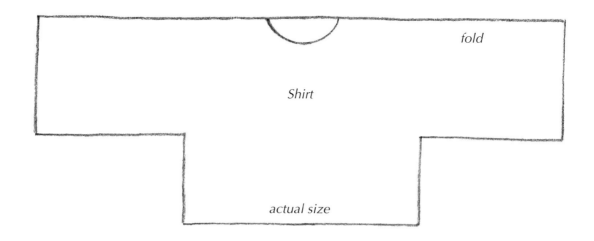

fold

Shirt

actual size

Star children

MATERIALS
See *Flower girl with legs*
Yellow felt for dress and star headdress
Yellow silk for the apron

Make the body according to the instructions for *Flower girl with legs,* head circumference 2 3/4 in (7 cm).

Cut the dress out of yellow felt, sew up the sides and sleeves and gather the neck and sleeve endings.

Cut a 3 7/8–4 1/4 in (10–11 cm) long and 2 3/4 in (7 cm) wide piece of yellow silk for the apron. Fold it in half lengthways and cut a hole for the neck opening. Pull it over the doll's head and gather the neck. At the same time hem the top edge, as silk unravels easily. Fold the shoulder edges inwards and sew the apron to the dress with a few stitches under the arms. You do not need to sew the folded edge.

Cut the star crown out of yellow felt and put it on the star child.

Star child with trousers

MATERIALS
See *Flower girl with legs*
Yellow felt for the suit and star crown

Make the body following the instructions of the Flower girl with legs, head circumference 2 3/4 in (7 cm). It is not necessary to put cotton knit over the legs.

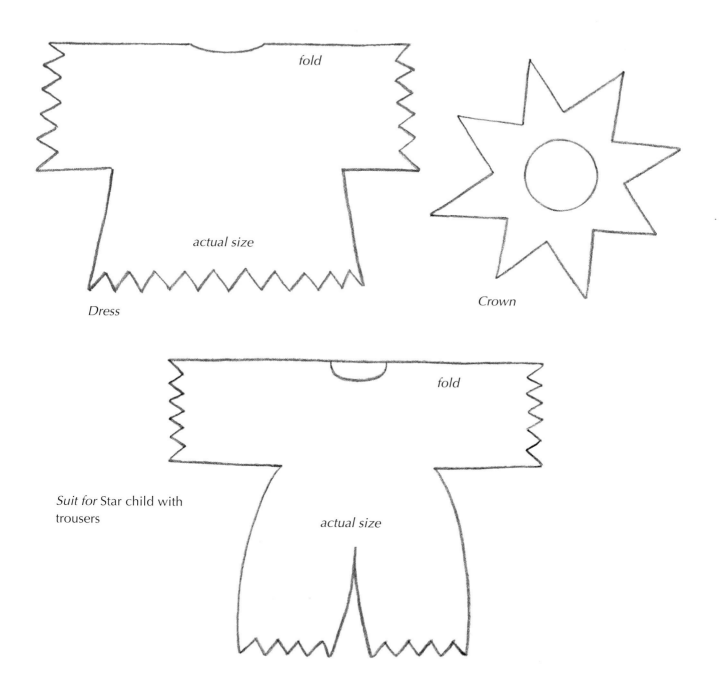

fold

actual size

Dress

Crown

Suit for Star child with trousers

fold

actual size

57

Cut the suit out of yellow felt and sew it together.

To make cotton knit feet, follow the instructions for the hands.

Now put the suit on from below and gather at the neck, the sleeve endings and the ankles.

Bend the feet forwards.

Cut the star crown out of yellow felt and put it on the head.

Small star child

MATERIALS
See *Star child with trousers*

Make the star child according to the instructions for *Star child with trousers,* head circumference 2 in (5 cm).

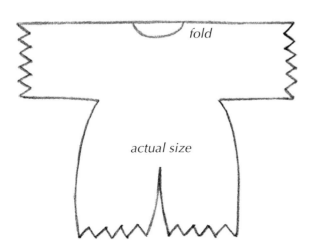

Suit for Small star child

Crown for Small star child

Autumn

In autumn, life begins to draw back again and people become more inward. It is a time when we start to meet in front of the seasonal tableau again. The main characters at this time of year are not so much flower children, but small gnomes; some visible, some invisible. Sometimes we find a crystal or feather on the season table that one of these beings brought with them. Our children also build beautiful gnome realms for their little friends outside in the garden or woods.

Gnome with spade

MATERIALS
See *Flower boy with legs*
Felt for clothes and hat, colour of your choice
Possibly coloured magic wool for the feet
Scraps of fur for hair and beard

Make the body according to the instructions for *Flower boy with legs*, head circumference 2 3/4 in (7 cm). This gnome has a small nose which you can make following the instructions for forming the face (page 19).

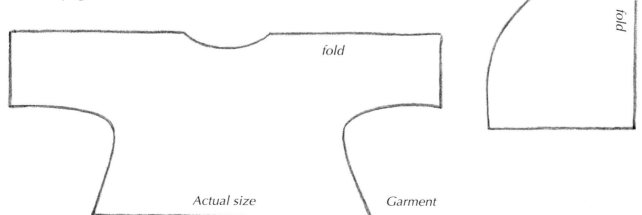

Trousers

Hat

fold

fold

Actual size *Garment*

Sew the garment and turn it right way out. Make the trousers according to the pattern for the Flower boy with legs. Pull both garments over the legs onto your gnome. Shorten the legs so that the trousers have to be pushed up 3/8 in (1 cm). Remember to allow 3/4 in (2 cm) for the feet first. Gather the lower edge of the legs, push them up to the right length and sew them in well through the sheep's wool of the legs. Make felt boots for the feet. Alternatively, you can wind coloured magic wool tightly around the feet.

Make the beard and hair out of real fur separated from the leather and glue it on well.

Sew the hat with buttonhole stitch and stretch it if necessary to fit the hair.

Blue gnome

MATERIALS
See *Flower boy with legs*
Blue velour for the suit and hat

Make the body according to the instructions for Flower boy with legs, head circumference 2 3/4 in (7 cm).

Make the suit out of blue velour. Use the pattern for *Star child with trousers* (page 56), but do not cut the pointed endings. Cut out the hat and fit it to the head and hair volume of the gnome. Sew the hat together and turn it right side out. Sew it to the front of the head while folding in a small hem.

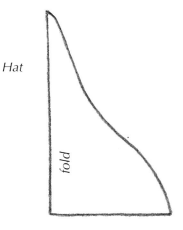

Hat

fold

Root gnome

MATERIALS
See *Flower boy with legs*
T-shirt fabric for the under-smock
Brown felt for the hat, over-smock and trousers
Thin string

Make a body according to the instructions for *Flower boy with legs,* head circumference 2 ³/₄ in (7 cm). Make the gnome an under-smock out of T-shirt fabric. Leave a seam allowance at the sleeve endings and gather them at the same time as sewing in the raw edge.

Cut the over-smock out of brown felt and pull it over the gnome's head. Now tie off the over-smock just under the arms with a piece of thin string.

Make the hat and trousers out of brown felt. Wind brown magic wool around the feet.

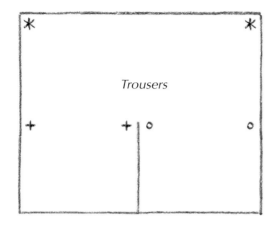

Trousers

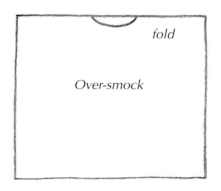

Over-smock

fold

Actual size

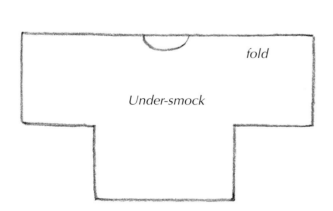

Under-smock

fold

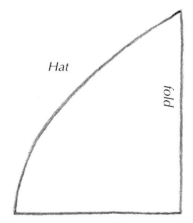

Hat

fold

Gnome with lichen beard

MATERIALS
See *Flower boy with legs*
Coloured felt for the clothes
Small wooden bead
Lichen or moss for the hair and beard

Make the body according to the instructions for *Flower boy with legs*. Head circumference 2 in (5 cm). Only tie off the eye line.

Use lichen or moss for hair.

Make the clothes according to the pattern for *Grass child* or *Corn child* (pages 36 or 72).

This example shows that it is possible to use suitable natural materials for hair.

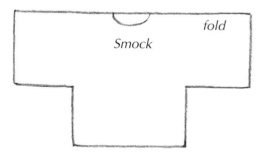

Smock

fold

Actual size

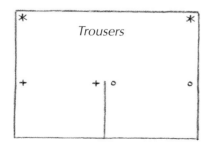

Trousers

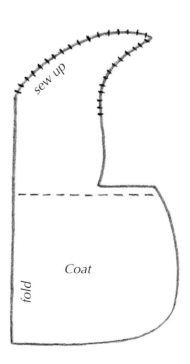

sew up

fold

Coat

65

Moss gnomes

Sock wool in shades of green
Knitting needles size 11 (3 mm)
Cotton knit, unspun sheep's wool, wool
  remnants
Mohair for the hair and beard

Knit the gnome according to the following pattern:
Cast on 20 stitches
Knit 12 rows
Bind off 4 stitches on either side
Purl 10 rows

For the hat decrease one stitch either side, knit one row, decrease one stitch either side, knit one row etc. Sew the hat together with small stitches.

Wind a small ball out of unspun sheep's wool about 3/4 in (2 cm) circumference and proceed according to the instructions for the other heads. Tying off the eye line is quite difficult, but worth it. You do not need to tie the chin line. You can also sew a small nose as described in the basic patterns. Push the finished head into the hat and gather a thread around the neck. Now sew the coat shut at the front and stuff some unspun sheep's wool into the gnome from below.

Make the hair and beard out of mohair. To do this, sew loops right around the face. Fasten the loops to the outer stitches of the coat and hat. Cut the loops open and trim the beard and hair to the desired length.

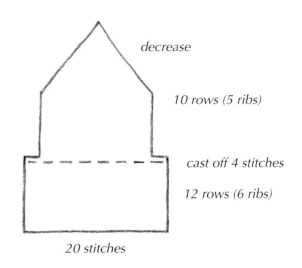

decrease

10 rows (5 ribs)

cast off 4 stitches

12 rows (6 ribs)

20 stitches

Field bindweed child

MATERIALS
See basic pattern for the *Flower girl with long skirt*
White felt for the dress and flowers
Florist's wire, 7 3/4 in (20 cm) for the stalk, 2 3/4 in
   (7 cm) for the leaf and 3 in (8 cm) for the bud
Thin craft wire
Florist's tape or green felt for winding around the stalk
Green felt for the leaves

Flower child

Make the body and dress according to the instructions for *Flower girl with long skirt,* head circumference 3 in (8 cm).
   Make the dress out of white felt.

Flower and stalk

Cut 5 petals out of white felt. Lay two of the petals on top of each other and sew one side together with buttonhole stitch. Now place the third petal onto the second petal and again sew one side to the other with buttonhole stitch. Repeat this process with the remaining petals, sewing the side of the last petal to the side of the first petal. Make sure the seam is facing outwards on all petals. To make the seam in the centre of each petal, turn the flower round, fold the petal lengthways and sew the fold with buttonhole stitch. Repeat with each petal. You should now have a trumpet shaped flower with alternating inward and outward buttonhole stitch seams. Pull the felt apart a bit at the top of the flower.

Take a single piece of florist's wire for the stalk (rather than the usual double) and wind florist's tape or green felt around it. Remember to wind the leaf stalk and the bud stalk to the main stalk.

To do this, place the wires together and wind around both for 3/8 in (1 cm).

To make the pistil in the centre of the open flower, cut 3 pieces of craft wire 1 1/4 in (3 cm) long and wind white thread around them. Fold these wound wires in half, place them at the top end of the stalk and wind thread around the stalk and pistil wires. Push the flower over the pistil and stalk end and wind white thread tightly around the base. Now bend the pistils apart.

Cut the two heart-shaped calyx leaves out of green felt and sew them briefly at the top and bottom with the pointed end towards the flower. The wide end should be on the stalk, the pointed end against the flower. If the two 'hearts' are too far apart, glue them together.

Cut the closed bud out of white felt and wind it into a cylinder. Twist this cylinder two to three times and fasten it with a few stitches. Push the bud onto the stalk which you have covered with 3/8–3/4 in (1–2 cm) of glue. Make the calyx as described for the flower.

Cut the leaf out of green felt and embroider the veins with green embroidery thread. Sew it slightly overlapping to the leaf stalk.

To make the creepers, wind a piece of green craft wire around the stalk twice and wind the 1 1/2 in (4 cm) end around a pencil or ball-point pen refill. Remove it carefully.

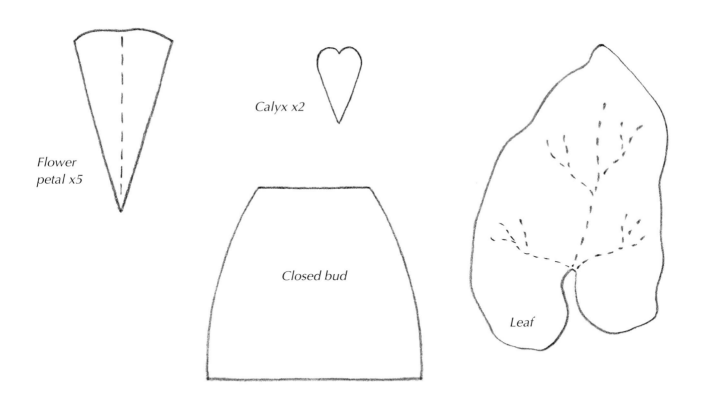

Flower
petal x5

Calyx x2

Closed bud

Leaf

Chestnut child

MATERIALS
See *Flower girl with long skirt* for dress and body.
Brown felt for the dress
Green felt for the cloak and hat

Make the body and dress according to the instructions for *Flower girl with long skirt,* head circumference 3 in (8 cm).

Cut the cloak out of green felt and fold it in half. Sew a seam along this central fold from top to bottom. This gives the cloak the shell-like look of a chestnut. The seam should be on the inside of the cloak. Now gather around the outside of the entire chestnut cloak and pull the thread slightly. Fasten it left and right at the shoulders and in the middle of the lower dress hem. Sew the hat out of the three pieces with seams inwards. Fit it to the head size and stretch or make it smaller depending on the hair.

To finish, take a small needle and roughen a small surface of the cloak felt. You can now twist the roughened patch into a tiny spine. Repeat this process over the entire cloak and hat to make the chestnut spines. If you find it difficult making the spines pointed, use some craft glue.

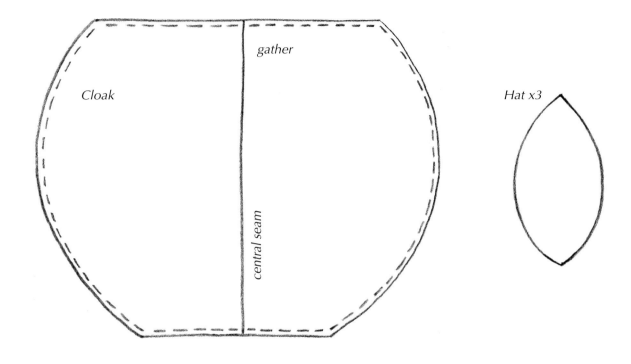

gather

Cloak

central seam

Hat x3

Actual size

Chinese lantern flower child

MATERIALS
See *Flower boy with legs*
Orange felt for smock, trousers and cloak
Florist's wire
Small wooden bead
Chinese lantern flower

Flower child

Make the body, smock and trousers according to the instructions for *Flower boy with legs,* head circumference 2 3/4 in (7 cm). Make the smock and trousers following the pattern for the *Grass*

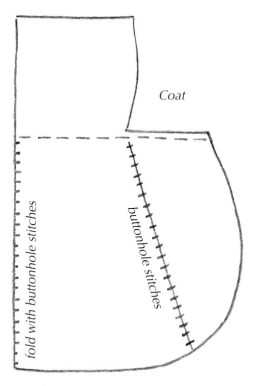

Coat

fold with buttonhole stitches

buttonhole stitches

Actual size

child (page 36). The hair is made out of wool fur fabric.

Cut the coat out of orange felt. Fold the coat in the middle and sew a buttonhole stitch seam along this fold from the bottom to start of the hood. Sew the side seams in the same way. The seams should be on the outside. Sew the hood (seam inside). Gather the neck, put the cloak on the doll and pull the thread until the two side edges meet. Sew the two edges together at the top with a few stitches. Fasten a wooden bead to the top as a button.

Make light green felt slippers for the feet.

Stalk

Take a doubled, twisted piece of florist's wire for the stalk, finished length 3 in (8 cm). Fasten the Chinese lantern flower to this stalk. Place the real Chinese lantern flower stalk beside the wire stalk and wind around them both for 3/4 in (2 cm) with florist's tape or green felt. To finish, carefully bend down the top of the stalk.

Corn child

MATERIALS
See *Flower boy with legs*
Light brown felt
1 ear of corn
Small wooden bead
Wool fur fabric for hair

Make the body according to the instructions for *Flower boy with legs,* head circumference 2 3/4 in (7 cm). Use wool fur fabric for the hair. Make the smock, coat and trousers according to the pattern for *Grass child* (page 36).

Cut the coat out of light brown felt, but do not cut the arm holes. Sew up the hood, turn the coat and gather at the neck. Put it on the doll and pull the thread to the right width. The edges should not overlap, leave a small gap. Fasten the coat left and right at the neck with a few stitches. Sew the wooden bead to one side as a button. Make the slippers out of light brown felt.

Shorten the stalk of the ear of corn to about 5 7/8 in (15 cm) and place it in the flower child's arm.

Toadstool children

MATERIALS
For body and dress, see *Flower girl with long skirt.*
White felt for the dress and toadstool cap underside
Red felt for the toadstool cap

Large toadstool child

Make the body and dress according to the instructions and pattern for *Daisy child* (page 32), head circumference 2 in (5 cm). Only tie off the eye line. Make the hands out of a circular piece of cotton knit. Pull these tightly over the pipe-cleaner arms and tie off at the wrists with a double thread.

For the toadstool cap, cut a circle out of red felt for the top, and a circle out of white felt for the underside. Sew both circles together with buttonhole stitch along the outer edge. Cut the inner circle out of the white felt with a sharp, small pair of scissors. Fill the toadstool cap with some unspun sheep's wool and then glue it to the head of the toadstool child. Now glue the white felt dots to the red cap.

You can make different toadstools or mushrooms, e.g. champignons, by using the appropriate colours for the cap.

Small toadstool child

Make the head of the small toadstool child 1 1/2 in (4 cm) in circumference. Make the head as for the large toadstool child. Sew the smock together with buttonhole stitch, but do not turn right way round. Now proceed as described for the large toadstool child.

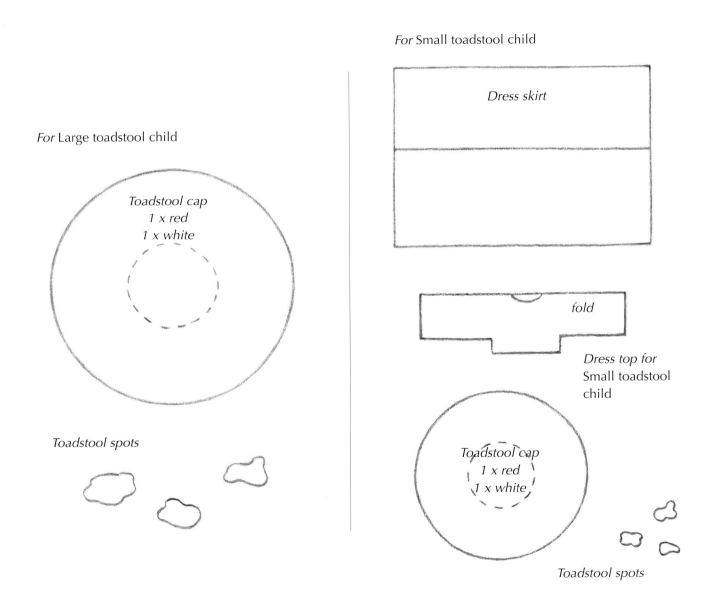

For Small toadstool child

Dress skirt

fold

Dress top for Small toadstool child

For Large toadstool child

Toadstool cap
1 x red
1 x white

Toadstool spots

Toadstool cap
1 x red
1 x white

Toadstool spots

Leaf child

MATERIALS
See *Flower boy with legs.*
Brown felt for the suit
Acorn hat or beechnut shell

Make the body according to the instructions for *Flower boy with legs.* Make the head circumference 1 3/4 in (4.5 cm), arm length 2 3/8 in (6 cm). Only tie off the eye line. Sew a piece of magic wool to the head for hair, matching in colour to the suit. You can trim the hair if desired.

Cut the suit out of felt.

Sew the suit together with buttonhole stitch and put it on the doll over the legs.

Make the hands out of two circular pieces of cotton knit pulled tightly over the wound pipe-cleaner endings. Tie off the wrists with a double thread and push the remaining cotton knit into the sleeve.

Wind unspun sheep's wool around the feet for shoes.

Glue the leaf child's stomach to a dry autumn leaf and put an acorn hat or beechnut shell on its head.

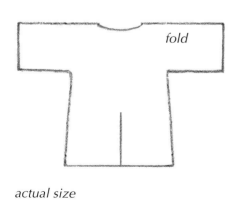

fold

actual size

Hazelnut boy

MATERIALS
See *Flower boy with legs.*
Medium brown felt for trousers, jacket and hat
Green felt for the smock

Make the body according to the instructions for *Flower boy with legs,* head circumference 2 3/4 in (7 cm). Use the *Grass child* (page 36) pattern for trousers and smock.

Make the smock out of green felt and the trousers out of medium brown felt. Cut the arm-holes carefully, if necessary enlarge them later. Try the jacket on the doll. If it is too big, make it smaller. The jacket should be open at the front. Cut a fringe into the lower edge and twist the strands between your fingers to resemble hazelnut leaves.

Fold the hat together in the centre and sew buttonhole stitch along the curve. Turn the hat right way round. Depending on hair volume stretch the hat.

Give the hazelnut child a real hazelnut to hold in its hand.

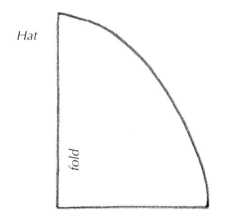

Hat

fold

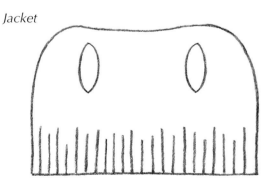

Jacket

Winter

Winter brings weather that is freezing, damp or chilly. While the forces of nature are very subdued, it is still a beautiful and exciting time for children. They can play outside for hours or go sledging. And when they come back, freezing cold and with a red nose, or soaked to the skin, they can sit cosily at the nature table.

The table is kept more or less bare, in keeping with the season, while the snowflake and snowdrop children encourage storytelling or singing.

Snowman

MATERIALS
White, short staple, slightly greasy unspun
   sheep's wool
Some red magic wool
Strand of wool for the hair
2 pipe-cleaners, each about 2 3/4 in (7 cm)

Wind three not too tight balls out of the unspun sheep's wool. The lower body ball should be 10 5/8 in (27 cm) circumference, the upper body ball 9 3/4 in (25 cm) and the head ball 7 1/2 in (19 cm). Sew the balls together by pushing a strong thread right through both body balls, sewing it in well, and then making the balls stable with a few stitches where they meet. Make sure the visible stitches disappear below the wool surface. Cut the lower ball so that the snowman can stand.

Sew eyes, mouth and buttons with black thread. Make the nose out of a small strand of red magic wool sewn to the nose space, twisted to make a pointy nose.

Wind magic wool lightly around the pipe-cleaners for the arms. Make sure the pipe-cleaners are also covered at the front end. Fasten the arms to the shoulders with a few stitches.

Wind the strand of wool loosely around three fingers to make the hat. Take this tapering tube off your fingers and sew it together at the back. Pull the upper end of the hat back a bit and sew it tight. Then sew the hat to the head with small stitches.

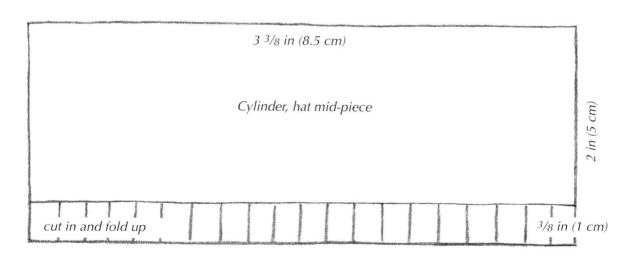

3 3/8 in (8.5 cm)

Cylinder, hat mid-piece

2 in (5 cm)

cut in and fold up

3/8 in (1 cm)

You can also make a hat out of thin cardboard instead of wool. Cut out the pieces according to the pattern, then cut the incisions, bend them up and glue them to the hat. To do this, first glue the mid-piece together at the back, push it up through the brim and glue the bent up pieces from below to the brim. Now glue the lid of the hat in place.

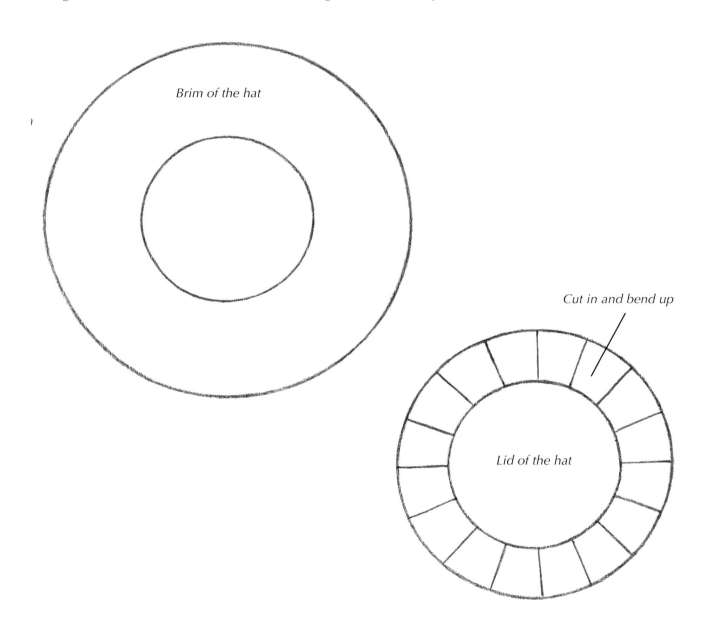

Brim of the hat

Cut in and bend up

Lid of the hat

Sledger

MATERIALS
See *Flower girl with legs.*
Light cotton knit for the head
Coloured cotton fabric for the dress
White cotton fabric for the long underpants

Make the body according to the instructions for *Flower girl with legs*, head circumference 2 3/4 in (7 cm). Use light cotton knit for the head to suit the time of year. Follow one of the hair patterns in the basic instructions for hair. To make the hat, follow the hat instructions for the *Skier* (below).

You do not have to cover the legs with cotton knit as the doll is wearing long underpants.

For the dress, follow the pattern described for the *Snowdrop girl* (page 87), but make it out of cotton fabric. You can also follow one of the patterns for the other flower girls (see Summer chapter).

Make the long underpants out of cotton fabric. Turn in the raw edges while gathering the stomach and legs.

Skier

MATERIALS
See *Flower boy with legs.*
Light cotton knit for the head
Different wool remnants for jumper and trousers
2 wooden lollipop sticks for the skis
Wooden skewers (kebab sticks) and thin card-
   board for ski sticks

Skier

Make the body as described for the *Flower boy with legs*, head circumference 2 3/4 in (7 cm). As for the sledger, use light cotton knit for the head. You can make the hair style as you please.

Before knitting/crocheting, measure your doll exactly and adapt the following patterns to fit your doll.

Knit the jumper out of knitting yarn. See the pattern overleaf for the exact size. Start the jumper at the bottom with '1 stitch plain, 1 stitch purl'. Then sew it together, turn right side out and put it over the body from below.

Crochet the hat. Make the bottom edge slightly larger than the head. After 1/2 in (1.5 cm) start decreasing regularly. Sew a few strands of wool to the top to make a tassel. The finished hat is 1 1/4 in (3 cm) long.

Single crochet the trousers, leg length 3/4 in (2 cm), entire length 1 1/2 in (4 cm). Sew the trousers together as described in the basic pattern *Flower boy with legs.* Now put the trousers on.

Skis

You can either buy the skis from a doll's shop or make them yourself. To do this, take two lollipop sticks and fasten two 3/8 in (1 cm) wide elastic bands to the centre of them to hold the boots. The elastic band should be short enough to hold the boots tight. Glue the elastic band to the underside of the sticks.

Make the ski sticks out of two wooden skewers. Shorten them to the length of your doll's shoulder height. Do not cut the pointed side. Cut two small circles out of thin cardboard and pierce a hole in the centre of them both with a needle. Push the circles onto the sticks and glue them just above the pointed end. Sew the ski sticks to the doll's hands.

Trousers

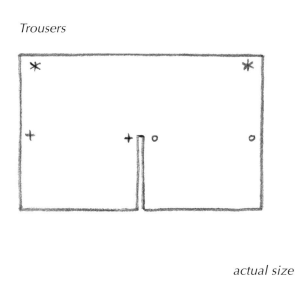

actual size

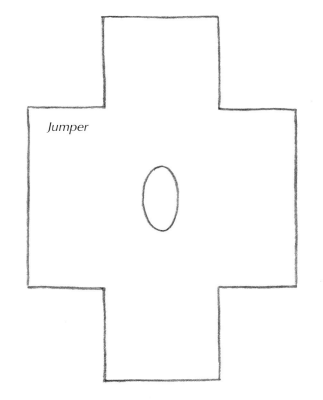

Jumper

Snowflake child (small)

MATERIALS
Stuffing wool (unspun sheep's wool)
White or skin-coloured cotton knit
White silk remnants or white wool fur fabric
Wool

Make a head about 1 1/2 in (4 cm) circumference. To do this, wind a ball about 1 3/8 in (3.5 cm) circumference. For a doll this small, you do not need eye or chin lines.

Cut a circle out of silk, gather it close to the edge and pull the thread tight to make a ball.

Fill this ball with some unspun sheep's wool and push the head into it. You might need to shorten the hanging down bits of cotton knit. Pull the gathering thread tight and sew in the ends well.

Cut the 'icicles' out of silk and gather them close to the edge. Wind this silk piece around the snowflake's neck (single or double) and cut off the end. Sew in the gathering thread to the dress.

Sew some short staple white sheep's wool to the head for hair. Now gather a short strip of 'icicles,' pull it tight and sew it to the hair. If you want to hang up the snowflake child, fasten a double thread to the top of the head.

To make a snowflake child out of wool fur fabric, make the head as described above. Follow the same pattern for the wool fur fabric body as for the silk snowflake child. Do not add 'icicles' to this doll, but make a hat following the pattern below. Sew the back seam last to fit the hat to the head. Sew the two half circles together and then gather them slightly.

To hang up, fasten a double thread to the top of the head.

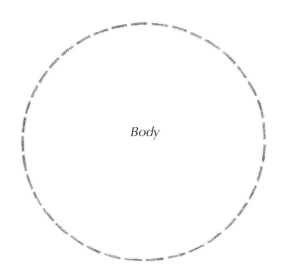

Body

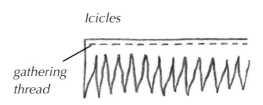

Icicles

gathering thread

make as long as you wish

Catkin children on a branch

MATERIALS
Light grey velour
Pipe-cleaner

Make a head 1 1/2 in (3–4 cm) circumference. You do not need to tie off eye and chin line. Cut the pieces of fabric hanging down from the neck to 3/16 in (0.5 cm).

Cut the dress out of velour, fold it in half, sew it together and turn right way out.

Stuff the dress lightly and put the neck through the neck hole. Gather the neck and sew in the gathering thread well. Push a 1 3/4 in (4.5 cm) long pipe-cleaner through the sleeves, bent around at the hands. Use a circle of cotton knit to cover the hands. Place the cotton knit over the hands, pull it tight and wind a double thread around the wrists a few times to hold it tight. Sew in the thread.

Cut the hood out of velour. Sew it together at the top and turn it around. Sew the hood from shoulder to shoulder to the dress (right side to right side). Pull the hood over the head and fasten the hood to the head with a few stitches.

Stitch the fringe to the head with white thread.

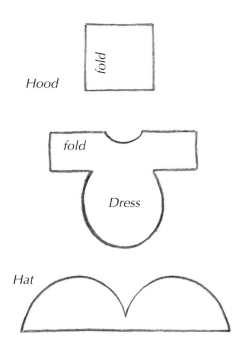

Catkin child

MATERIALS
See *Flower child with long skirt* for body and dress.
White and brown felt
Florist's wire
About 4 real catkins

Flower child

Make the body and dress according to the instructions for *Flower girl with long skirt,* head circumference 3 in (8 cm). Use white felt for the dress. Make a stomach strip according to the pattern below and fasten it around the stomach. Use the same pattern for the sleeve endings.

Catkin stalk

Wind brown felt around the 6 ¼ in (16 cm) long florist's wire for the catkin stalk. Bend the stalk in four places and glue the catkins to the bends. Cut four brown felt calyxes following the pattern below.

Remember there are smaller and bigger catkins, you might have to adjust the patterns to suit the size. Lay the calyx around the bottom end of the catkin and sew it to the stalk.

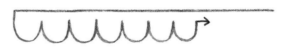

see stomach circumference

Calyx

85

Large Snowdrop child

MATERIALS FOR THE FLOWER
White felt
Green felt
Florist's wire for the stalk
Small white glass beads

Flower child

Make the body and dress according to the instructions for *Flower girl with long skirt*, head circumference 3 in (8 cm). Use white felt for the dress.

Cut out the collar, place it around the neck and sew it together at the back with a few stitches. Glue a white small glass bead to each point of the collar.

Flower and stalk

Make the snowdrop stalk out of florist's wire, finished length 5 1/2 in (14 cm).

Twist the wire together, leaving a small loop at the top to hang the snowdrop on. Wind florist's tape or green felt tightly around the stalk.

Cut out the white petals and glue the 'inner flower' piece of felt together into a tube, slightly overlapping (opposite). This is easy to do if you pull the felt over the sharp edge of a pair of nail scissors. This also gives it the right shape. Gather the 'flower' piece at the top and pull the thread until the 'flower' evenly encircles the 'flower inside.' Sew in the thread by sewing 4–5 buttonhole stitches over the top edge through the flower parts. Make sure that the flower is curved, not straight. Do this by sewing the top edges together with two buttonhole stitches, then pushing them

together and sewing another two buttonhole stitches into the first two.

Cut the calyx out of green felt and glue it around the top edge of the flower. Again sew it as described above to make a curve. Do not cut the thread, but use it to fasten the flower to the stalk. Pull the thread through the small loop at the top of the stalk. Do not pull the thread tight, but leave 1/32 in (1 mm) so the flower can swing back and forth. Sew 3–4 buttonhole stitches around the thread and then sew it in.

Colour the flower centre slightly yellow and the outside lower edge of the petals slightly green.

Bend the stalk over so that the flower can hang downwards. Glue the small seed-leaf to the bend. Sew the larger leaves to the bottom of the stalk.

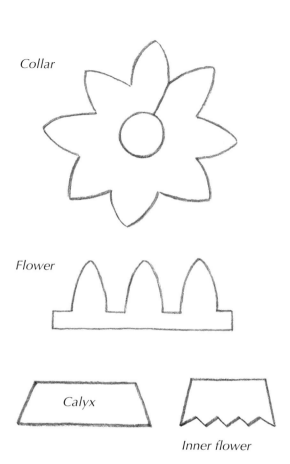

Collar

Flower

Calyx

Inner flower

Leaves

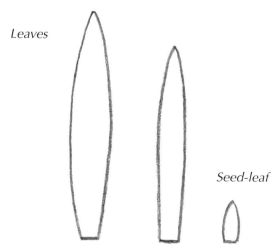

Seed-leaf

Snowdrop girl with legs

MATERIALS
White cotton knit fabric, e.g. of a white T-shirt
White felt
Green felt
Florist's wire for the stalk
Small white glass beads

Flower child

Make the body and dress according to the instructions for *Flower girl with legs*, head circumference 2 3/4 in (7 cm).

Use white T-shirt fabric for the dress (cotton). See *Different children* for the pattern (page 53).

Use the lower, hemmed edge of the T-shirt for the hem. Cut out the pieces twice, sew them together and turn the dress right way out. Put it on the doll from below. Gather the neck and sleeves, at the same time narrowly hem the edges.

Flower and stalk

Make the stalk and flower the same as for the large snowdrop child.

The Nature Corner

Celebrating the year's cycle with seasonal tableaux

M. van Leeuwen and J. Moeskops

Seasonal nature tables are an invaluable way of making young children aware of the changing cycle of the year. With simple materials a series of colourful and effective tableaux can be made at home or in school for depicting the seasons and major festivals.